Walking on Water with St. Peter

Reflections to Strengthen Your Faith

D1563448

Giuseppe Agostino

Translated by
Marsha Daigle-Williamson, PhD

Published by The Word Among Us Press
7115 Guilford Drive, Suite 100
Frederick, Maryland 21704
www.wau.org

17 16 15 14 13   1 2 3 4 5

ISBN: 978-1-59325-223-6
eIBSN: 978-1-59325-448-3

Cover design by John Hamilton Designs
Cover photo: Getty Images

Library of Congress Control Number: 2013940543

CONTENTS

Introduction

꿎

Behold, I am laying in Zion for a foundation
a stone, a tested stone. (Isaiah 28:16)

He was called Simon. He was Jona's son and Andrew's brother. Both brothers were fishermen on the Lake of Tiberias. They had met Jesus, heard his call, and followed him, leaving everyone and everything behind. One day when Jesus arrived in the region of Caesarea of Philippi, he asked his disciples what people thought about him. He received various answers. Jesus continued, "But who do you say that I am?" Simon Peter replied, "You are the Christ, the Son of the living God" (Matthew 16:15, 16).

What a revelation! In professing Jesus as the Messiah, Peter added the profession of his divine sonship; he considered Jesus the Son of God, the living God.

He had already made that profession with the other disciples who were with him when their boat was being buffeted by the wind. At Jesus' word, the wind had ceased, and they prostrated themselves and exclaimed, "Truly you are the Son of God" (Matthew 14:33).

When he personally recognized Jesus as God's Son, Simon had a mysterious christening. Jesus said to him, "Blessed are you, Simon Bar-Jona! For flesh and blood has not revealed this to you, but my Father who is in heaven. And I tell you, you are Peter, and on this rock I will build my Church, and the gates of Hades shall not prevail against it. I will give you the keys of the kingdom of heaven, and whatever you bind on earth shall be bound in heaven, and whatever you loose on earth shall be loosed in heaven" (Matthew 16:17-19).

In changing Simon's name, Jesus indicated that he was a foundational stone for the building of his Church. The word *petros* in Greek and the corresponding Aramaic word *kefa* (rock) had never been used for people's names before Jesus gave that name to the fisherman from Bethsaida.

Peter has always fascinated me. I have always been struck by his spontaneity, his enthusiasm, his weakness, his generous and openhearted nature, and his deep and passionate, tried-and-tested faith. However, the name Jesus assigned him—Peter from "rock"—is attractive to me on a deeper level.

In his first epistle, Peter will develop a kind of theology about the concept of "stone" when he says,

Come to him, to that living stone, rejected by men but in God's sight chosen and precious; and like living stones be yourselves built into a spiritual house, to be a holy priesthood, to offer spiritual sacrifices acceptable to God through Jesus Christ. For it stands in Scripture:
> "Behold, I am laying in Zion a stone, a cornerstone chosen and precious,
> and he who believes in him will not be put to shame."
To you therefore who believe, he is precious, but for those who do not believe,
> "The very stone which the builders rejected has become the cornerstone,"
and

"A stone that will make men stumble,
a rock that will make them fall." (1 Peter 2:4-8)

I like thinking of Peter as a "living stone" and hearing about his life and his teaching so that I, too, can become a "living stone," together with all the brothers and sisters of faith, and be built together as a Church.

In the Bible, a stone or rock not only represents solidity but also, paradoxically, among the wonders of God, a fountain of life. The Book of Numbers records the following mysterious words of the Lord during a time of thirst in the desert: "The LORD said to Moses, 'Take the rod, and assemble the congregation, you and Aaron your brother, and tell the rock before their eyes to yield its water; so you shall bring water out of the rock for them; so you shall give drink to the congregation and their cattle'" (20:7-8). Deuteronomy describes the desert for Israel as "thirsty ground where there was no water," but for the people of Israel, the Lord brought "water out of the flinty rock" (8:15).

In his First Letter to the Corinthians, Paul speaks about Israel's journey, which is an image of the Church's journey, and notes, "All drank the same supernatural drink. For they all drank from the supernatural Rock which followed them, and the Rock was Christ" (10:4). Christ is the rock, the cornerstone, and Peter is its sign.

I like approaching Peter this way, as a rock from which the water of life can flow. I will look at what Peter has to tell us through his words, his actions, his responses—and resistance—to what Jesus gave him and asked of him.

The result is illuminating because the head of the Apostolic College, Peter's successor, is a solid rock for us. If it rains, if rivers overflow, if the winds blow and shake the house, the house will not fall because it is built on rock (Matthew 7:25). We are all "living stones," but Peter and his successors are living stones in a unique way.

I will present brief meditations on passages in which Peter either appears, speaks, or acts, using three major sources in sequence: the Gospels, Acts of the Apostles, and Peter's letters. This is not a book of exegesis or theology but of spirituality. I will present a biblical passage and then a meditation on its application for our lives today—a time of so much blossoming despite so much aridity.

Peter is the first to call himself a "living stone" so that all of us, through his example and teachings, can become living stones through which the Church is always made more solid and alive. May he be a solid rock through which the water that gives life and quenches thirst can gush forth.

Giuseppe Agostino
Metropolitan Archbishop Emeritus
Cosenza–Bisignano, Italy

1. THE CALL

❦

As he walked by the Sea of Galilee, he saw two broth-ers, Simon who is called Peter and Andrew his brother, casting a net into the sea; for they were fishermen. And he said to them, "Follow me, and I will make you fishers of men." Immediately they left their nets and followed him. And going on from there he saw two other brothers, James the son of Zebedee and John his brother, in the boat with Zebedee their father, mending their nets, and he called them. Immediately they left the boat and their father, and followed him. (Matthew 4:18-22)

Jesus walked on the same paths that the people walked. Luke's Gospel, recording his encounter with the disciples at Emmaus, says, "While they were talking and discussing together, Jesus himself drew near and *went with them*" (Luke 24:15, empha-sis added).

In Exodus, there is an important dialogue between Moses and the Lord. Moses asks God,

"Show me now your ways, that I may know you and find favor in your sight. Consider too that this nation is your people." And [God] said, "My presence will go with you, and I will give you rest." And he said to him, "If your pres-ence will not go with me, do not carry us up from here. For how shall it be known that I have found favor in your sight, I and your people? Is it not in your going with us, so that we are distinct, I and your people, from all other people that are upon the face of the earth?" (Exodus 33:13-16)

God's walking alongside us demonstrates his love for us. He walks among us and "sees" us. Our text says that as Jesus was walking by the Sea of Galilee, he "saw" Peter and Andrew (Matthew 4:18). The Book of Job says that the eyes of God "are upon the ways of a man, / and he sees all his steps" (34:21).

The phrase "he sees" is profoundly significant. All of a person's life—his or her history, failures, and searching—is seen by Jesus. We could say that a person's whole spirituality is summarized in his becoming aware of being "seen" by Jesus. To be "seen" means to feel ourselves loved, accompanied, sought after.

Jesus saw Peter and his brother Andrew while they were casting their nets into the sea. He spoke to them and entered into their lives, not to deprive them of anything, but to transform their lives. Jesus asked them to follow him and promised to make them "fishers of men" (Matthew 4:19).

"Follow me," he says. What does this mean? Describing the crucified Lord in his first epistle, Peter will say, "Christ also suffered for you, leaving you an example, that you should follow in his steps" (1 Peter 2:21). The Book of Revelation says that the companions of the Lamb "follow the Lamb wherever he goes" (14:4).

Following Jesus does not mean that the Christian life consists in ideological adherence to him or in a mystical detachment from normal life. It means there is a "path" that retraces the footsteps of Christ the Master.

From one point of view, the life of Jesus cannot be repeated. But from another point of view, his life consists of footsteps that he left us so that we can see them and walk in them. To be a Christian means to walk in the footsteps of Jesus.

Jesus announced to Peter and Andrew God's plan for them: to be fishers of men. What does that mean? Human beings are frequently like people who are drowning and submerged by many things. We often need to be "fished out" to return to the truth and the breath of the life of God.

What a great mission it is to fish for men! But how much passion and how much energy that requires of us! No one has the right to hook the life of another human being and reel that person in for his or her own sake. It is enormously important for every worker in the mission field of the Church to understand the saying, "I will make you fishers of men." Every apostle, then, is acting in the name of Christ.

Peter and Andrew responded to the forceful, radical proposition from Jesus. The Gospel tells us how they responded, and their response is the archetype for the way we should all respond.

There are three facets in their response that we need to consider and continue to affirm in our own lives: "Immediately they left the boat and followed him" (Matthew 4:22).

"Immediately" implies that every delaying calculation, every attitude of holding back, can block a genuine following of Jesus. We cannot serve two masters, the Lord said (Matthew 6:24). Accepting Jesus as Master is like being blinded by a lightning bolt. We need to pray and ask him to reveal his face to us. Psalm 4:6 notes, "There are many who say, 'O that we might see some good! / Lift up the light of your countenance upon us, O Lord!'"

Peter and Andrew followed him and "left the boat." What does this mean? It does not mean becoming paupers and depriving ourselves of everything. On the contrary, it means possessing all things, not as though they belonged to us, but by making use of them with a profound interior detachment. A genuine Christian makes use of everything but is not enslaved to anything or anyone.

"Following Jesus" is thus not a quest for one's identity or one's gifts. It means having our egos disappear to discover ourselves following *behind* Jesus: "A disciple is not above his teacher" (Luke 6:40).

Peter's story begins with his serious radical detachment and with following Jesus. Despite times of fear and confusion, Peter would always be reenergized for service by the power of the Holy Spirit, even to the point of martyrdom. As such, he is an archetype of Christian life. ✑

2. "Follow Me and I Will Make You Fishers of Men"

೦

O ne time when Jesus was with them, there was such an extraordinary catch of fish that the boats were almost sinking. The Evangelist Luke tells us this:

> [Peter] was astonished, and all that were with him, at the catch of fish which they had taken; and so also were James and John, sons of Zebedee, who were partners with Simon. And Jesus said to Simon, "Do not be afraid; henceforth you will be catching men." And when they had brought their boats to land, they left everything and followed him. (5:9-11)

Peter was afraid, not only because of what he lacked spiritually, but also out of astonishment at the abundance of the catch. God manifests himself in so many ways that we can say he is always manifesting himself to us!

We often see what appears, what surrounds us, only as the fruit of our own labor and hard work. But if we go beyond appearances and know how to look past them to who is acting in our lives, then our amazement increases. In this episode, generally called "the miraculous catch," the Gospel notes that everyone who was with Peter was struck with great astonishment because of the surplus of fish.

Their amazement indicates their marveling at God. The eyes of faith make us contemplate the wonderful deeds of God continually. Job says that God "does great things beyond understanding,

/ and marvelous things without number" (9:10). Let us recall the song from Mary's heart, God's most sensitive antenna: "For he who is mighty has done great things for me, / and holy is his name" (Luke 1:49).

Holiness does not involve perfectionism; at its core, holiness is joy and wonder. It is an understanding of the constant mysterious fatherly presence of God who protects us, accompanies us, and works in our lives. Sometimes we are aware of it only gradually and dimly. When people are not educated about their faith, they often consider "destiny" as the cause of unpleasant events, or they ascribe these events to so-called evil spells and curses. Today there is a recurring emphasis on the presence of the evil one, and it is true that he exists and operates. However, the eyes of faith primarily see in all things the action of God in our lives and in history: "If you confess with your lips that Jesus is Lord and believe in your heart that God raised him from the dead, you will be saved" (Romans 10:9).

Amazement is the result of looking at God's ways as we remain silent and adore him. It is notable, however, that amazement does not have to produce fear. The Gospels, as in the case of the miraculous catch, often repeat to us the very encouraging words of Jesus: "Do not be afraid." Psalm 118:6-7 says,

With the LORD on my side I do not fear.
    What can man do to me?
The LORD is on my side to help me;
    I shall look in triumph on those who hate me.

Exhorted not to be afraid, Peter was able to hear the positive message from God: from now on you will be a fisher of men. This is a surprising statement that leads to many questions. Where do people fish for men? In the sea of life, the sea of history, of course. Human beings living apart from God are like people who are drowning.

Where do people find the elixir of happiness? The heart suffers so many disappointments. Worldly possessions, pleasures, and appearances do not satisfy. People experience what Dante's profound insight describes: "After their meal, they are hungrier than before" (*Inferno* 1.99). Today's ideological or scientific propositions offer solutions that are actually empty and abstract, so people still have a need for authentic peace within.

The Lord's invitation to be fishers of men means to seek out people to love them, to open up paths of life for them—not by offering pietistic suggestions, but by offering the meaning of life. There is a certain kind of religiosity that is merely a small lifeboat that only leads to more drudgery. Faith, instead, is freedom, the daughter of truth. Faith is not an idea; it is Someone.

It is the Lord who commands winds and storms and fills the nets, but then he makes those kinds of nets irrelevant when he says that the real fish are human beings. Christ came for human beings; he is the Truth for human beings. He is not trying to restrict our abilities but is directing them, channeling them, leading us to the true meaning of peace and especially of companionship: "Take heart, it is I; have no fear" (Mark 6:50).

The wonderful conclusion of the text is important: "And when they had brought their boats to land, they left everything and followed him" (Luke 5:11). The Lord wastes nothing and uses everything. Everything has a meaning and a place. Even the boats—they cannot be left to drift away. A person's inner integration likewise gives order and measure to everything.

This is how the vocations of Peter and the others came about. They left everything, but not as though losing everything, and they followed him as though pursuing a quest. Following Jesus means to have him live again through our lives. It means leaving pipe dreams behind and not chasing after illusions, but following him who is the Way for everyone and for all things. ∽

3. Peter's Mother-in-Law

The Gospel says, "And when Jesus entered Peter's house, he saw his mother-in-law lying sick with a fever" (Matthew 8:14).

Peter was married and, of course, had a house. When Jesus called Peter to follow him, he left everything. Jesus was, in fact, about to make him the caretaker of a much larger family, his Church. Peter's house, his family home, was in Capernaum. Matthew's Gospel tells us that Jesus entered that very house and, according to tradition, he often did so.

One day when he is in that city, he sees Peter's mother-in-law lying in bed sick. The verb "to see" and the expression "he sees" often appear in the Gospels to indicate Jesus' attentive presence as we face so many human problems. The mysterious intensity of his presence reveals his gaze of love. Through that gaze, Jesus, the incarnated Word of God, demonstrates that he is not placing himself above or outside of human events but, instead, revealing himself as the eye of the God who is Love—for all people, for all of humanity.

Entering Peter's home, "he saw" Peter's mother-in-law in bed with a fever. Every situation has a mysterious value if it is lived in communion with the Lord and if we know that he is always present to us. In my home region of Calabria, we often hear the people say, "The Lord sees and provides." It is a very valuable spiritually to place every event of life under God's gaze. This means that nothing is useless or insignificant. God's gaze, revealed in Christ who "sees" the situations, brings a salvific value to events, rescuing them from futility and senselessness.

In this Gospel narrative, the sick woman is not the one who is seeking help. The gaze of Jesus occurs first; he comes to her rescue. Knowing ourselves to be seen by God means that we place every situation, every event, under his gaze as a potential opportunity for charity on our part and for redemptive action on God's part.

Jesus demonstrated this through his actions, through his gaze. Entering a home, he knows that in every family there are countless joys but also countless trials. Jesus touches the hand of the sick mother-in-law and her fever goes away. Fever has many causes and is the symptom of a disease. St. Augustine, transposing this to the spiritual level with great insight, says that the "fever" that Jesus wants to heal is our pride, our avarice, our lust, and so forth.

Peter's mother-in-law, now healed, gets up and begins to serve. Even this detail—noted by the Gospel writer—contains a wealth of teaching. Health, a gift from God like all of our strength, should be used for service. Every person should be a servant for the good of all. Wouldn't it be wonderful if we would all exchange the gifts God gives us?

Throughout this episode, Peter is silent, but I am sure it is from amazement. He observes Jesus' actions; later, he would also become present to human suffering. We can recall, for instance, Peter's healing of the lame beggar in Jesus' name at the gate of the Temple (Acts 3:1-10).

More than anything else, however, Peter is growing as a disciple. And as a disciple, we know that he will, in fact, perform acts of charity for others, teaching them to put all their gifts in service to others. ∞

4. "DEPART FROM ME, FOR I AM A SINFUL MAN, O LORD"

∾

While the people pressed upon him to hear the word of God, he was standing by the lake of Gennesaret. And he saw two boats by the lake; but the fishermen had gone out of them and were washing their nets. Getting into one of the boats, which was Simon's, he asked him to put out a little from the land. And he sat down and taught the people from the boat. And when he had ceased speaking, he said to Simon, "Put out into the deep and let down your nets for a catch." And Simon answered, "Master, we toiled all night and took nothing! But at your word I will let down the nets." And when they had done this, they enclosed a great shoal of fish; and as their nets were breaking, they beckoned to their partners in the other boat to come and help them. And they came and filled both the boats, so that they began to sink. But when Simon Peter saw it, he fell down at Jesus' knees, saying, "Depart from me, for I am a sinful man, O Lord." (Luke 5:1-8)

Psalm 51, which is called the "Miserere," is a wonderful, down-to-earth prayer that is open to the hope that "does not disappoint us" (Romans 5:5). The psalmist confesses, "Behold, I was brought forth in iniquity, / and in sin did my mother conceive me. / Behold, you desire truth in the inward being" (51:5-6). He goes on to affirm, "A broken and contrite heart, O God, you will not despise" (51:17b).

The scribes and Pharisees brought to Jesus a woman taken in adultery. According to the Mosaic law, the woman should have been stoned, but Jesus said, "Let him who is without sin among you be the first to throw a stone at her" (John 8:7b). The Church tells us to pray to Mary—Jesus' mother conceived without sin—in this way: "Pray for us sinners."

Sin is a legacy that we all inherit, but Christ is "the Lamb of God, who takes away the sin of the world" (John 1:29b). The remission of sin is like the renewal of creation; it is the work of God.

The disposition that opens us to forgiveness is the admission of our sins. John summarizes this in a very clear and inspiring way: "If we say we have no sin, we deceive ourselves, and the truth is not in us. If we confess our sins, he is faithful and just, and will forgive our sins and cleanse us from all unrighteousness. If we say we have not sinned, we make him a liar, and his word is not in us" (1 John 1:8-10).

Salvation is a gift of God, but it requires a heart that is open to his mercy as we admit our sins. In the example of the prodigal son, the young man who gave himself over to debauchery is saved when he says, "I will arise and go to my father, and I will say to him, 'Father, I have sinned against heaven and before you; I am no longer worthy to be called your son'" (Luke 15:18-19). Jesus revealed the Father to us at this point with a profound truth that summarizes our faith in the God who saves: "But while he was yet at a distance, his father saw him and had compassion, and ran and embraced him and kissed him" (15:20).

Peter shows himself already affected by the spirit of salvation and is speaking as a genuine believer. Seeing the marvels of the Lord in the miraculous catch, he tells Jesus, "Depart from me, for

I am a sinful man, O Lord" (Luke 5:8). Acknowledging that we are sinners is the predisposition for receiving salvation.

I like to listen to Peter again and again, the leader and teacher of the Church, as he makes this statement, which has such mystical significance and indicates an experience of salvation. For centuries when we have approached Christ in the Eucharist, the Church has had us repeat the centurion's saying: "Lord, I am not worthy that you should enter under my roof, but only say the word and my soul shall be healed" (cf. Matthew 8:8). Today that house is our hearts.

True salvation begins when we understand that we need forgiveness. True prayer is humble. Peter acknowledges that he is a sinner and asks the Lord to depart from him. His confession involves recognizing the holiness of Christ and our unworthiness to receive him.

Today's world has lost a sense of sin. People do not recognize a need for forgiveness, so sin is trivialized. People are unaware of what sin is. Secular humanism and pragmatism consider sin a lack of commitment to social or political projects and a lack of responsibility in growing our bank accounts. There is no longer any amazement at the gifts of God, and there is no longer any openness to forgiveness. Self-sufficiency closes human beings not only to God but also to others.

Peter's thought-provoking statement demolishes the pride that exalts us and that divides us from one another. The gospel is not there to support our demands and our mental, political, and social constructs. It challenges us, instead, to open ourselves humbly to the God who saves and to open ourselves to others, since we are all in need of reconciliation and forgiveness. ∽

5. JESUS AND PETER WALK ON THE WATER

Then he made the disciples get into the boat and go before him to the other side, while he dismissed the crowds. And after he had dismissed the crowds, he went up into the hills by himself to pray. When evening came, he was there alone, but the boat by this time was many furlongs distant from the land, beaten by the waves; for the wind was against them. And in the fourth watch of the night he came to them, walking on the sea. But when the disciples saw him walking on the sea, they were terrified, saying, "It is a ghost!" And they cried out for fear. But immediately he spoke to them, saying, "Take heart, it is I; have no fear."

And Peter answered him, "Lord, if it is you, bid me come to you on the water." He said, "Come." So Peter got out of the boat and walked on the water and came to Jesus; but when he saw the wind, he was afraid, and beginning to sink he cried out, "Lord, save me." Jesus immediately reached out his hand and caught him, saying to him, "O you of little faith, why did you doubt?" And when they got into the boat, the wind ceased. And those in the boat worshiped him, saying, "Truly you are the Son of God." (Matthew 14:22-33)

This Gospel text is quite intriguing and suggestive. The enigma of God and the fears of human beings are both present. In particular, the humanness of Peter's emotions and his impatience appear without fanfare, but we also see his great sincerity of heart.

Jesus sends his disciples away, asking them to wait for him on the other side of the lake. Having also dismissed the crowd, he climbs up a mountain alone to pray.

This passage emphasizes that Jesus came to the disciples at night. He shows us the balance we need between spending time with others and spending time alone with God. Jesus was teaching us the secret of life according to God: do not always be with the crowd and do not always be isolated. People do not meet God if they do not meet other people, but it is even more important to emphasize that without an encounter with God, people run away from themselves and others.

Jesus, praying alone on the mountain, has had many imitators in the desert saints and in such places as Trappist and Carthusian monasteries. Unfortunately, the idea of solitude has largely slipped away today because of an overemphasis on social interaction and an unhealthy anthropology of human beings.

In this text, I am struck by the fact that Jesus did not take his disciples with him. Perhaps he did not believe they were mature enough for the silence that can be far more difficult than action. Perhaps he wanted to show us both sides of the coin that are expressed in St. Benedict's *ora et labora*, "pray and work."

In any case, Jesus is in a peaceful state of solitary prayer while the disciples are exhausted as they steer a boat that is being buffeted by winds. Toward the end of the evening—which means the beginning of the new day—Jesus moves toward them, "walking on the sea" (Matthew 14:26). No one can walk on water without sinking; human beings need solid ground to be able to walk.

The disciples' thinking was limited because they were not yet completely open to the faith through which everything is possible.

They did not recognize Jesus and thought that he was a ghost. How many times prideful logic finds refuge in the unreal! But faith overcomes fear and puts a face on others and gives meaning to things. Fear can rise up when we feel alone or helpless. It is while his disciples are in this state that Jesus reveals himself.

This Gospel, which is very terse in its exposition and does not multiply words, simply expresses it this way: "Immediately he spoke to them, saying, 'Take heart, it is I; have no fear'" (Matthew 14:27). "Immediately" means a redemptive readiness on his part as he sees their state of confusion and bewilderment. "Spoke" does not so much mean he opens his mouth as that he reveals himself. The Gospels frequently record Jesus saying, "It is I." In doing so, Jesus reveals himself as the Absolute "I Am," outside of whom no one is saved. Next, he says, "Have no fear." What a wonderful statement! It is interesting to examine what our fears are and where they come from. We can say, in general, that fears come from the isolation of our egos.

At this point in the episode, Peter takes the initiative and says, "Lord, if it is you, bid me come to you on the water" (Matthew 14:28). Apparently, he had not yet recognized the Lord's face, and he was looking for a sign. Jesus tells him to come, and Peter leaves the boat and begins to walk on the water. Did he get that power from Jesus? Certainly in an act of faith there is the power of God to overcome human impossibilities. Humanly speaking, though, faith is overcome by fear when the "I" cuts itself off from the power of God and submits to the limitations and powers of nature.

In line with his spontaneity and exuberance, Peter cries out, "Lord, save me" (Matthew 14:30). Jesus reaches out to him and says, "O you of little faith, why did you doubt?" (14:31). Doubt is like a worm that eats away at faith.

Faith means entrusting oneself confidently to the power of God that surpasses all human potential. A storm may cause faith to rise up, but it can also diminish faith. When Jesus gets into the boat with Peter, the wind ceases. The disciples prostrate themselves before Jesus and exclaim, "Truly you are the Son of God" (Matthew 14:33). I am struck that this profession of faith in Jesus is also made by Peter (cf. 16:16). This belief will solidify, and Peter and his successors will sustain the faith of the Church.

Faith brings the power of God into the midst of our many human weaknesses. ◡

6. "EVERYONE IS SEARCHING FOR YOU"

∽

The Evangelist Mark, who was a disciple of Peter, records a moment in Jesus' ministry when Jesus secretly leaves Capernaum and goes to Galilee. Mark writes,

> And in the morning, a great while before day, he rose and went out to a lonely place, and there he prayed. And Simon and those who were with him followed him, and they found him and said to him, "Every one is searching for you." And he said to them, "Let us go on to the next towns, that I may preach there also; for that is why I came out." (1:35-38)

Jesus would often leave without telling his disciples in order to pray in deserted places. Prayer in Jesus' earthly life was the most significant expression of his union with the Father and of his passion for human beings. Prayer, the source of everything for him, took priority over everything else.

There is a lesson for all of us here, especially when we have serious responsibilities or very troubling problems. We often ask, "What are we going to do?" and then perhaps we do not pray. Action should never be the priority: "And do not seek what you are to eat and what you are to drink, nor be of anxious mind. For all the nations of the world seek these things; and your Father knows that you need them. Instead, seek his kingdom, and these things shall be yours as well" (Luke 12:29-31).

We need to withdraw to reconnect with ourselves. What kind of prayer was Jesus engaged in when he went away from everyone and everything? Paul gives us the answer when he says, "Pray at all times in the Spirit, with all prayer and supplication. To that end keep alert with all perseverance, making supplication for all the saints" (Ephesians 6:18).

Prayer, then, does not occur at a particular time; it is not the recitation of a formula. It is a continuous habit; it is a communion of ongoing love in the Holy Spirit. Jesus loved deserted places, not so that he could be alone, but so that he could be joined with everyone, seeing them as they are in the Father and in the Holy Spirit.

Simon and the others set about to find him, and finding him, they tell him, "Every one is searching for you" (Mark 1:37). This statement is a comment about all human beings.

Some people today consider God to be the great "Absent One," and there are those who talk about "the silence of God." But this is not really the way things are. Who God is constitutes the greatest and most burning question for all human beings. This universal search for God is the real and radical issue that is common to all human beings. It is implicitly the search for truth, peace, fellowship, and joy:

But I am poor and needy;
　　hasten to me, O God!
You are my help and my deliverer;
　　O LORD, do not delay! (Psalm 70:5)

Peter, the guide for believers of all times, tells us that everyone is looking for Jesus. Today a disciple is not someone who acts and accomplishes things but someone who knows that God is not dead and that he is not the great "Absent One." He is what human beings hunger and thirst for.

To find God we have to seek him. We need to rechannel our tensions, our stresses, and our energy. If we chase after feelings, success, and appearances, we will be drawn into the void sooner or later. People who seek God feel themselves loved and sought after. Nevertheless, we will never fully possess him on earth:

> My tears have been my food
>   day and night,
> while men say to me continually,
>   "Where is your God?" (Psalm 42:3)

The issue of God is the provocative and mysterious question for every human being.

I believe the Church can undergo changes, and new attitudes can arise, but what does not change is that people will always be looking for God and will always be sought by him. Peter realized this in embryonic form. Jesus made him understand this when he said, "Let us go on to the next towns, that I may preach there also; for that is why I came out" (Mark 1:38). That is what he came for—for all human beings, for all places, for all times. Christ is, yesterday, today, and forever, for everyone. ❧

7. JESUS' TRUE RELATIVES

In Mark's Gospel, Jesus says, "Your mother and your brethren are outside, asking for you" (3:32). They are called "brethren," or in some translations "brothers," not because they are sons of Mary, but because they are close relatives like cousins. In Hebrew and Aramaic, these kinds of relatives are called "brothers."

Jesus was informed that Mary and other relatives wanted to talk to him. In a mysterious, piercing divine flash, he asks the messenger, "Who are my mother and my brethren?" (Mark 3:33). Then pointing to his disciples, he says, "Here are my mother and my brethren! Whoever does the will of God is my brother, and sister, and mother" (3:34-35).

What a statement, and what an astounding understanding of parentage and kinship! The word "parent," from *parens,* implies shared genetics. We all have relatives—parents, brothers, sisters, and so forth—to whom we are connected through biology. But the revelation we get from this thought-provoking and suggestive text is that we now transcend the boundaries of biological relationships and enter into a new family.

We are all children of the same heavenly Father. We call him "Our Father," and that phrase indicates our having been born from above. This is why the world is, or at least should be, one family. In the passage we are meditating on here, Jesus, after being told that his relatives are there, points to his disciples as if he were instituting and creating something new: "Here are my mother and my brethren" (Mark 3:34).

The disciples heard this statement as one revealing a new truly radical and inclusive family. As Christians, we have "new" relatives who, as John says, "were born, not of blood nor of the will of the flesh nor of the will of man, but of God" (1:13). Christians are born from above. We are made "perfectly one" (17:23) and "firm in one spirit" (Philippians 1:27). We have "one faith, one baptism" (Ephesians 4:5).

Peter, in this new family, passed on the wonderful name of "Holy Father" to his successors, the supreme pontiffs of the Church. Peter and his successors are the signs of this genealogy in the Holy Spirit, the signs of a new family among human beings based on a genealogy that comes from above. The apostles, and Peter in particular, are the vehicles of divine life and are sacraments of the fatherhood of God.

This is the way the transformation of human relationships is presented in the Gospel: "Call no man your father on earth, for you have one Father, who is in heaven" (Matthew 23:9). Peter, as well as his successors, is a sign of fatherhood that comes from above and makes the Church a sacrament of Christ, according to the Second Vatican Council. It is a sign and an instrument of intimate union with God and of the unity with the whole human race. *Lumen Gentium* refers to this new family relationship when it says that the "duty of the church [is] that all people, who nowadays are drawn ever more closely together by social, technical, and cultural bonds, may achieve full unity in Christ." ∽

8. THE TAX PAID BY PETER

Matthew's Gospel records this episode about the Temple tax:

> When they came to Capernaum, the collectors of the half-shekel tax went up to Peter and said, "Does not your teacher pay the tax?" He said, "Yes." And when they came home, Jesus spoke to him first, saying, "What do you think, Simon? From whom do kings of the earth take toll or tribute? From their sons or from others?" And when he said, "From others," Jesus said to him, "Then the sons are free. However, not to give offense to them, go to the sea and cast a hook, and take the first fish that comes up, and when you open its mouth you will find a shekel; take that and give it to them for me and for yourself." (Matthew 17:24-27)

This episode in Jesus' life, which seems to be a private conversation between Jesus and Peter, incorporates many simple yet profound teachings. The tax collectors at Capernaum approach Peter to ask about payment of the tax. This involves an issue that is hardly ever preached about or emphasized: Jesus was faithful to the norms of civil and religious common life concerning taxes. His engagement with the human race made him "a citizen of the world." He taught us to render to God what is God's and to Caesar what is Caesar's (cf. Matthew 22:21).

There are often many valid reasons to withdraw from our civic duties. Despite those reasons, Jesus pointed to solidarity and did not appeal to the privileges and rights, for example, of religious exemption. Believers should not avoid their civic duties. They should not seek exemptions but be motivated to fulfill their duties and be aware of the common good.

The fact that there are legitimate secular duties is often discussed today, and faith can shed light on such duties. This discussion is very important and deserves to be pursued so that we avoid becoming "tax dodgers in God's name." We should, as believing citizens, especially as lay Christians, do our part when the laws are just and authentically seek the common good.

The conversation between Jesus and Peter reveals that we need to avoid giving offense in the controversies that can arise about this or that duty or right. Scandal, I believe, does not occur only inside politics. It can also occur in regard to the poor, the so-called invisible ones, with whom we are called to share. When we speak about "giving offense," through ingrained habit we often generally refer to instances of sexual misconduct or a dereliction of duties. This can often be the case, but when Jesus says in this text "not to give offense" (Matthew 17:27), he is referring to tax evasion and teaching us about doing our civic duties without seeking exemptions.

Within God's all-knowing provision, there was a shekel in the mouth of the first fish Peter found. Jesus goes on to say, "Give it to them for me and for yourself" (Matthew 17:27). This is wonderful because it shows that Providence supports and helps us in fulfilling our duties. This sign introduces a factor that can help motivate our civic behavior: the mystery of Providence is at work with our faith so that our conduct is irreproachable in all things.

In the apostolic succession, the pontiffs, especially in recent times, have highlighted certain social issues, and we are grateful to the Lord for that. However, I am certain that the thrust of their teaching involves our action. Let us remember that Jesus, in a full and comprehensive way through so many aspects of his life, showed us how to live: "I have given you an example, that you also should do as I have done to you" (John 13:15). ∽

9. NOT SEVEN TIMES BUT SEVENTY TIMES SEVEN

ᴄ⁓

This saying in the Semitic language refers to one of the strongest commandments that characterize Christian life: forgiveness. Peter, perhaps affected by his own experience, approaches Jesus and says to him, "Lord, how often shall my brother sin against me, and I forgive him? As many as seven times?" Jesus replies, "I do not say to you seven times, but seventy times seven" (Matthew 18:21, 22).

In the earliest centuries of the life of the Church, bishops asked three questions when they interviewed catechumens for admission to baptism: Did they understand the mystery of the cross? Were they open to selling their goods to help the poor? Were they capable of forgiving all offenses?

Forgiveness is a traditional Christian concept. It comes to us from contemplating our Master, Jesus, whose first words when he was being crucified in the place called the Skull were "Father, forgive them; for they know not what they do" (Luke 23:34). All of Jesus' life consisted of forgiveness. Paul writes to the Corinthians, "Christ reconciled us to himself and gave us the ministry of reconciliation" (2 Corinthians 5:18). Peter not only transmitted Jesus' saying about always forgiving, but he also personally experienced the forgiveness of the Lord after his betrayal.

The Second Vatican Council affirms:

The Church encompasses with her love all those who are afflicted by human misery and she recognizes in those who are poor and who suffer, the image of her poor and suffering Founder. She does all in her power to relieve their need and in them she strives to serve Christ. Christ, "holy, innocent and undefiled" (Hebrews 7:26), knew nothing of sin (2 Corinthians 5:21), but came only to expiate the sins of the people (cf. Hebrews 2:17). The Church, however, clasping sinners to her bosom, at once holy and always in need of purification, follows constantly the path of penance and renewal. (*Lumen Gentium*, 8)

I like to meditate on "seventy times seven," not just in terms of the number of sins to forgive, but also as a lifestyle for believers as we deal with secularism and atheistic humanism and with those who are called "instruments" of sin. The Church has never cooperated with sin but is always corrective of it.

Sin produces violence, war, political wrangling, broken families, sexual license, and so forth. As a Church, we can often feel bewildered, but the idea of "seventy times seven" that Peter heard is conveyed to us in many ways so that we do not lose heart because of so many "structures" of sin. We remember that God makes the sun shine on the righteous and on the wicked every day and that his mercy endures forever.

Thus, the Church is not dismayed but always purifies itself deeply through its members to announce the hope of reconciliation and to affirm and demonstrate, despite the world's confusion, that "God is greater than our hearts" (1 John 3:20). ∽

10. A Surprising Reward

Matthew's Gospel records Peter asking Jesus this question: "Behold, we have left everything and followed you. What then shall we have?" (19:27). Then Jesus replies,

"Truly, I say to you, in the new world, when the Son of man shall sit on his glorious throne, you who have followed me will also sit on twelve thrones, judging the twelve tribes of Israel. And every one who has left houses or brothers or sisters or father or mother or children or lands, for my name's sake, will receive a hundredfold, and inherit eternal life. But many that are first will be last, and the last first." (Matthew 19:28-30)

This is both a human and a divine text; it is very rich because it teaches something significant and enlightening. Peter, a sincere and forthright man who had left everything to follow Jesus, asks an understandable question. Peter was also asking the question on behalf of the other disciples: "What then shall *we* have?" (Matthew 19:27, emphasis added). In doing so, he was already demonstrating an initial conversion because he was no longer speaking in the singular but in the plural; he already knew he was part of a community. This is the new language for Jesus' followers, language that in its later theological and cultural development will lead to the phrase "episcopal collegiality."

Was Peter's question worldly and pragmatic? I do not think so. The question could have been phrased this way: "What will happen to us? What nonmonetary reward will we receive?" Jesus had already taught his followers about poverty and detachment from worldly goods. Peter's question here comes from a human perspective. Jesus answers with enigmatic and lofty words. He primarily defines the mysterious dimension into which they are following him as "the new world"; he refers to them as "you who have followed me" into this new world (Matthew 19:28).

What does that mean? This dense expression has immense implications. It offers a perspective and vision beyond time, since "the new world" has its complete fulfillment only in the next life. It exists but is not yet definitive. This new world will become visible from time to time during Jesus' life on earth.

Jesus speaks explicitly about the next world and its fulfillment, its definitive outworking. However, there is already on earth the seed of this new creation—through an encounter with Christ. When Christ calls us, we are called to new life. "Truly, truly, I say to you, unless one is born anew, he cannot see the kingdom of God" (John 3:3). John adds, "That which is born of the flesh is flesh, and that which is born of the Spirit is spirit" (3:6).

Jesus is describing the ultimate judgment on everyone and everything. He reveals himself as the judge of history who will reward every gift from human beings. Jesus realizes that following him involves many renunciations, but he offers himself as the inheritance and fullness of life.

This passage in which Peter asks this important question ends with these words from the Lord: "But many that are first will be last, and the last first" (Matthew 19:30). God's yardstick is not the yardstick of human beings. His loving eye does not see appearances but hearts. He does not see according to the limitations of human beings but according to his own truth. ∽

11. THE CALLING OF THE TWELVE

༄

Among the synoptic Gospels that describe the commission-ing of the Twelve, I have chosen Mark's Gospel because of its terseness and profundity and because of Mark's personal con-nection with Peter.

> And he went up on the mountain, and called to him those whom he desired; and they came to him. And he appointed twelve, to be with him, and to be sent out to preach and have authority to cast out demons: Simon whom he sur-named Peter; James the son of Zebedee and John the brother of James, whom he surnamed Boanerges, that is, sons of thunder; Andrew, and Philip, and Bartholomew, and Mat-thew, and Thomas, and James the son of Alphaeus, and Thaddaeus, and Simon the Cananaean, and Judas Iscariot, who betrayed him. (Mark 3:13-19)

Great things always come from above because they are gifts from God. The Gospel says that Jesus, before his important deci-sions, always climbed a mountain. A mountain is the part of the earth closest to the sky; it demonstrates the tension of stretching toward the divine.

Solitude is necessary for authentic communion. We should all rediscover Jesus on the mountain and the spirituality that flows from that silent encounter. Without silence first, there are no authentic words. If we do not listen to God, there is no word from him for us. The selection of the Twelve, a very significant event for the life of the Church and human history, occurred as a result of contemplation.

Jesus "called to him those whom he desired" (Mark 3:13). In that short verse, there are two irreducible truths about every vocation—it is God who calls; it is not our choice. Our part is in answering the call. Every calling is a definitive, mysterious gift from God; it is an expression of his will. There are moments when we vaguely and sometime trivially attribute unpleasant events in our lives to being God's will, and this may indeed be the case at times. But God's will is not always some mysterious force that acts against us. God's will is a love that draws, creates, re-creates, and lifts up. Every act of God's will is a free action flowing from his love that selects and opens up new paths for us.

The Gospel says, "They came to him" (Mark 3:13). It seems to me that this is like an embrace. God chooses out of love and they respond out of love. Every vocation is a response to God's eternal initiative that appears in a specific time and place.

Jesus appoints the Twelve. That number is a sign of unity in diversity, of universality in multiplicity. The number twelve recalls the twelve tribes of God's chosen people. The calling of the Twelve is very thought provoking and significant because their call is "*to be with him,* and to be sent out to preach and have authority to cast out demons" (3:14-15, emphasis added). It seems that the radical meaning of their call is "to be with him," and that their being with him is the source of their preaching and freedom from the evil one.

This remarkable text frees us from what has been called "the heresy of action." There can be no significant action without an authentic inner life. It is profound communion with God that opens the way for communion with other people. The Italian priest Don Oreste Benzi used to say, "You can stand ready on the front lines for humanity if you are on your knees before God."

Preaching is the first missionary activity. To preach is to speak about God, to proclaim his mystery, to reveal his face. People's fears cannot be exorcised by coddling them. People need, instead, to know as they are known, to love as they are loved. To cast out demons is to free the human heart from the wiles of the evil one and to strengthen souls against temptations to evil.

Mark then lists the names of the Twelve. In naming the first one, he calls him by his original name, Simon, but adds, "whom he surnamed Peter" (Mark 3:16). In naming the last one, Judas Iscariot, Mark adds the comment "who betrayed him" (3:19). Any of us can be a betrayer so we all need to pray, "Deliver us from the evil one and do not lead us into temptation."

We always stand on *super firmam petram*, on "solid rock," as we contemplate the first disciple who was listed. Simon, who was given the name Peter, forever represents a solid rock for us. ❧

12. "ON THIS ROCK I WILL BUILD MY CHURCH"

The key passage about Peter, his faith, and his initial mission is found in Matthew's Gospel:

Now when Jesus came into the district of Caesarea Philippi, he asked his disciples, "Who do men say that the Son of man is?" And they said, "Some say John the Baptist, others say Elijah, and others Jeremiah or one of the prophets." He said to them, "But who do you say that I am?" Simon Peter replied, "You are the Christ, the Son of the living God." And Jesus answered him, "Blessed are you, Simon Bar-Jona! For flesh and blood has not revealed this to you, but my Father who is in heaven. And I tell you, you are Peter, and on this rock I will build my Church, and the gates of Hades shall not prevail against it. I will give you the keys of the kingdom of heaven, and whatever you bind on earth shall be bound in heaven, and whatever you loose on earth shall be loosed in heaven." Then he strictly charged the disciples to tell no one that he was the Christ. (Matthew 16:13-20)

Jesus was not, as we say today, taking a survey. The mystery of Jesus is transcendent and eternal and cannot be treated on the level of numbers and statistics. The question he asks about himself is passed on by the Gospel writers to all of us.

Jesus initially asks his disciples what the people think about him rather than what they themselves think. He receives various responses that include the names of great spiritual figures who acted as reference points for the people of Israel: John the Baptist, Elijah, Jeremiah, or one of the prophets. Their answers indicate that the people were fascinated by these great men. Then Jesus wants to hear from his disciples—"Who do you say that I am?" (Matthew 16:15). In a certain sense, he is presenting the question to the Church that is still in embryonic form, the Church in gestation. Peter steps forth and delivers the penetrating answer for each person and for all of history: "You are the Christ, the Son of the living God" (16:16).

Jesus is the Christ, the Messiah, but not as an extraordinary figure or as a sign of God. He is God himself, the Son of the living God in the mystery of the Trinity. This truth—one that is uniquely Christian—is here proclaimed by Peter for all time. God is not a mere concept or a force that frees us from our needs. John says that he is the Word that "we have looked upon and touched with our hands," the life that "was made manifest" (1 John 1:1, 2). Paul says, "To me to live is Christ" (Philippians 1:21), and "It is no longer I who live, but Christ who lives in me" (Galatians 2:20).

Jesus confirms Peter's answer, calling him "blessed" (Matthew 16:17). He is blessed because his confession of Jesus as the "Son of the living God" is a revelation from above, from the Father in heaven. Through faith, Peter proclaims on behalf of himself and all others the great mystery that invests Jesus. Because of this, Jesus changes Peter's name. He is no longer Simon but Peter, because he will be the rock for the building of Christ's Church against which the powers of hell will be powerless.

Jesus is the Lord, and Isaiah says, "Only in the LORD . . . / are righteousness and strength" (45:24). Paul says, "Thanks be to

God, who gives us the victory through our Lord Jesus Christ" (1 Corinthians 15:57). God is the Father who waits, who is respectful even of our whims, but in the end he always has the last word.

After this confession of faith Jesus gives Peter the power to loose and bind. What is bound on earth will be bound in heaven and what is loosed will be loosed in heaven (Matthew 16:19). Human beings, then, are no longer slaves but free. In his first epistle, Peter will say, "Live as free men, yet without using your freedom as a pretext for evil; but live as servants of God" (1 Peter 2:16). Freedom, then, lies in knowing the truth.

Jesus then commands the disciples not to tell anyone that he is the Christ (Matthew 16:20). What does this command mean? It is highly significant. Scholars speak of "the messianic secret," which means that Christ, the One who saves, the Messiah, the anointed One of God, would become for many the rock of stumbling in the revelation of the cross. Jesus is saying that in order to accept him as the risen Lord, we will need to accept him as the crucified One.

We tend to welcome the resurrection but without the cross. Peter will explain the connection between the two in his first epistle: "But rejoice in so far as you share Christ's sufferings, that you may also rejoice and be glad when his glory is revealed. If you are reproached for the name of Christ, you are blessed, because the spirit of glory and of God rests upon you" (1 Peter 4:13-14). ∽

13. JESUS CALLS PETER "SATAN"

The Evangelist Matthew records the words of Jesus as he begins to talk openly about his approaching death and resurrection. This text deals with Jesus' explicit announcement of those events:

> From that time Jesus began to show his disciples that he must go to Jerusalem and suffer many things from the elders and chief priests and scribes, and be killed, and on the third day be raised. And Peter took him and began to rebuke him, saying, "God forbid, Lord! This shall never happen to you." But he turned and said to Peter, "Get behind me, Satan! You are a hindrance to me; for you are not on the side of God, but of men." (Matthew 16:21-23)

Peter's humanity erupts here as he protests to Jesus that this will never happen. It is an act of love on his part, but it is not enlightened. Peter was an emotional person; he could be enthusiastic or depressed. He confesses faith in Jesus, but he flees in the hour of Jesus' passion.

However, after the paschal event and in the light of Pentecost, Peter will decisively proclaim the paschal mystery to the large crowds. In Jerusalem he will give his first great sermon to the crowd and proclaim that Jesus was the one "you crucified and killed by the hand of lawless men." But he adds, "God raised him up, having loosed the pangs of death, because it was not possible for him to be held by it" (Acts 2:23, 24). He will earnestly emphasize, "This Jesus God raised up, and of that we all are witnesses" (2:32). Peter's successors throughout the centuries will proclaim that same mystery to crowds in the very square in Rome that bears his name.

All of Peter's ministry will unfold with the proclamation of God's victory over death, over every death. In the introduction to his first epistle, Peter will repeat that message: "Blessed be the God and Father of our Lord Jesus Christ! By his great mercy we have been born anew to a living hope through the resurrection of Jesus Christ from the dead, and to an inheritance which is imperishable, undefiled, and unfading, kept in heaven for you" (1 Peter 1:3-4).

For many people, the cross is often an obstacle and not a ladder to heaven. It is very useful for us to listen again to Jesus' strong words, which can apply to us as they did to Peter when he called him Satan: "You are not on God's side" (cf. Matthew 16:23).

The cross is a mystery that occurs in many facets of our lives: in our personal lives, in the lives of our families, in church life, in the great historical conflicts, in war. We can feel confused and broken. Jesus tells us, "You are not on God's side," and reproves us that we are still acting and thinking according to the spirit of Satan.

I think about how we often shape our lives according to our plans, our dreams, and our achievements with a deemphasis of the cross. Paul, who loved Jesus, tells the Corinthians, "Christ did not send me to baptize but to preach the gospel, and not with eloquent wisdom, lest the cross of Christ be emptied of its power. For the word of the cross is folly to those who are perishing, but to us who are being saved it is the power of God" (1 Corinthians 1:17-18). Paul goes on to say, "Jews demand signs and Greeks seek wisdom, but we preach Christ crucified, a stumbling block to Jews and folly to Gentiles, but to those who are called, both Jews and Greeks, Christ the power of God and the wisdom of God" (1:22-24).

It is when we accept Christ crucified and the implications of the cross for our lives that we are "on God's side." ∾

14. STUPEFIED AT TABOR

∾

Matthew the Evangelist says, "Jesus took with him Peter and James and John his brother, and led them up a high mountain apart" (17:1). Peter is always the first witness in the powerful events of Jesus' human-divine experiences. He will be the one to tell the Church and the whole human race about these events—first during his own life and, in the future, through his successors. It is noteworthy that the events in Peter's life that are highly significant for us are always accomplished by Jesus "apart."

Jesus, the man of mystery, does not seek applause but demonstrates humility to those who observe him. He prefers to have the light of God appear in silence, in the hidden things of the Spirit.

The episode that I call "stupefied at Tabor" is told to us in this way: "He was transfigured before them, and his face shone like the sun, and his garments became white as light" (Matthew 17:2). This marvelous fact reveals who Jesus is. He often appeared in his human aspect, but it was always illuminated by the divine. At other times, he appeared primarily in his divine aspect—his unutterable, inexpressible aspect.

In order to describe the Transfiguration and his change in appearance, the Gospel writer uses references to our experience: his face shone like the *sun* and his clothes like *light*. Jesus is "the light of the world" (John 8:12), and in him our light shines before others (Matthew 5:16; cf. 1 Peter 2:12).

In this scene, Moses and Elijah appear with Jesus and speak with him, but Jesus is the definitive Word. In him the ancient law and the prophets are fulfilled and transformed. The law and the prophets comprise the history of salvation up until this point, but now Jesus inaugurates the salvation of history.

At this point, Peter, the frank, straightforward, no-frills apostle, steps in and says, "Lord, it is well that we are here; if you wish, I will make three booths here, one for you and one for Moses and one for Elijah" (Matthew 17:4). He wants to fix forever this transcendent, luminous, significant moment.

"He was still speaking, when behold, a bright cloud overshadowed them, and a voice from the cloud said, 'This is my beloved Son, with whom I am well pleased; listen to him'" (Matthew 17:5). The bright cloud was like a mysterious light. A cloud can provide cover, but in this case it lit up the scene. Before the Sanhedrin who presumed to judge him and the high priest who asked, "Are you the Christ, the Son of the Blessed?" Jesus answered, "I am; and you will see the Son of man sitting at the right hand of Power, and coming with the *clouds of heaven*" (Mark 14:61, 62; emphasis added).

As they view this theophany and hear the voice from the cloud, the disciples fall on their faces, seized by great fear. Jesus makes them get up and says, "Rise, and have no fear" (Matthew 17:7).

Peter remained stupefied by the Tabor event. He was so captivated in his heart that he will affirm in his second letter, with bold faith, "We made known to you the power and coming of our Lord Jesus Christ, but we were eyewitnesses of his majesty. For when he received honor and glory from God the Father . . . , we heard this voice borne from heaven, for we were with him on the holy mountain" (2 Peter 1:16-18). Peter always carried Tabor in his heart.

The mountain with light dazzled him; the mountain with the cross confused him. But this is Peter's way. He will weep bitterly for his betrayal of Jesus (see Matthew 26:75), but he is a model of a sincere human being. Peter never ceased being a man—small but great, weak but decisive. As a model, he comforts us.

The text about Tabor ends this way: "When they lifted up their eyes, they saw no one but Jesus only" (Matthew 17:8). This verse points to the purification our eyes and hearts need: to see Jesus only, and in him to see ourselves, to see others, and to see the world and all of history. ∾

15. THE INDIGNANT DISCIPLES

Genuinely following Jesus is not easy. It requires continual detachment and a right disposition. Mark records the weakness of two brothers, James and John, the sons of Zebedee. They ask Jesus, from their worldly perspective, to be seated at his right hand and his left in his glory.

> They said to him, "Grant us to sit, one at your right hand and one at your left, in your glory." Jesus said to them, "You do not know what you are asking. Are you able to drink the chalice that I drink, or to be baptized with the baptism with which I am baptized?" And they said to him, "We are able." And Jesus said to them, "The chalice that I drink you will drink; and with the baptism with which I am baptized, you will be baptized; but to sit at my right hand or at my left is not mine to grant, but it is for those for whom it has been prepared." (Mark 10:37-40)

We cannot presume on God; everything is a gift from him. We are only required to be generously and constantly faithful.

In this episode, the Gospel says that the other ten disciples, including Peter, were "indignant" toward James and John (Mark 10:41). What was the reason for their indignation? Was it an appropriate reaction from pure hearts to the two brothers' request? Was it a judgment against the two presumptuous disciples, since the others were not approaching this issue in the same way? We do not know. The Gospel merely records their indignation.

Indignation is the opposite of tolerance and mercy. Jesus understood the limitations of the human heart; he came precisely because of our weaknesses. Paul tells the Corinthians that God "has shone in our hearts to give the light of the knowledge of the glory of God in the face of Christ" (2 Corinthians 4:6). However, "We have this treasure in earthen vessels, to show that the transcendent power belongs to God and not to us" (4:7). In reference to our condition, the word of God says, "The Spirit helps us in our weakness; for we do not know how to pray as we ought" (Romans 8:26).

Indignation means losing a spirit of mercy and especially of humility. People who have a spirit of mercy and humility know how to accept others and how to accept themselves. Jesus does not react to the disciples' indignation with another example of indignation but with the gift of truth. He says, "Whoever would be great among you must be your servant, and whoever would be first among you must be slave of all. For the Son of man also came not to be served but to serve, and to give his life as a ransom for many" (Mark 10:43-45).

In our experience as believers, we are often indignant when we see so many things that are wrong in the world. We also feel indignant when we see the limitations of the Church through the failings of its members. The Christian response is never to focus on the evils but to uproot them and bring forth the truth. When we have compassion for others, we are acting like Christians.

I want to note as well that systematic attacks against the Church by ideological or intra-ecclesial groups ordinarily do not come from people who love the truth but from dispirited, contentious people. Jesus, with great tenderness, gives us a clear and comforting response to this kind of situation when he says, "Blessed are you when men revile you and persecute you and utter all kinds of evil against you falsely on my account" (Matthew 5:11). ∽

16. THE DRIED FIG TREE:
FAITH AND PRAYER

c⌒o

Jesus was returning from his triumphant entry in Jerusalem where a very large crowd had been shouting "Hosanna" (Matthew 21:9). He spent the night in Bethany. The Gospel tells us, "In the morning, as he was retuning to the city, he was hungry" (Matthew 21:18).

In the episode of the fig tree, Peter is accompanying Jesus when he becomes hungry. The Master sees a fig tree along the way and approaches it, but he finds only leaves on it. Faced with its barrenness, Jesus gives a great teaching that is very valuable for us today as we face innumerable human problems. First, he dries up the fig tree. Jesus teaches his astonished disciples that as we face human needs for subsistence, there is a principle of life that animates nature itself and all social organizations: faith. He tells them, "Truly, I say to you, if you have faith and never doubt, you will not only do what has been done to the fig tree, but even if you say to this mountain, 'Be taken up and cast into the sea,' it will be done. And whatever you ask in prayer, you will receive, if you have faith" (Matthew 21:21-22).

The key to life is faith, but not a faith that is independent of or opposed to reason. Faith does not involve disengagement from life but a choice to move forward with action, not in our own power, but in the light and power of God. The centurion felt unworthy that Jesus should enter his house to heal his servant, saying, "Lord, I am not worthy to have you come under my roof" (Matthew 8:8). But the Lord said to him, "Go; let it be done for you as you have believed" (8:13).

It is not the shriveling up of a fig tree that can block us but the shriveling up of our hearts. In the incident with Jairus' daughter, Mark writes, "While he was still speaking, there came from the ruler's house some who said, 'Your daughter is dead. Why trouble the Teacher any further?' But ignoring what they said, Jesus said to the ruler of the synagogue, 'Do not fear, only believe.' And he allowed no one to follow him except Peter and James and John the brother of James" (Mark 5:35-37).

Peter, then, called to proclaim and to guard the faith of the brothers and sisters, is a witness that faith remains strong, "for he endured as seeing him who is invisible" (Hebrews 11:27). ∽

17. "Lord, To Whom Shall We Go?"

John tells us that Jesus spoke early on about the Eucharist, the Bread of Life, saying, "He who eats my flesh and drinks my blood has eternal life, and I will raise him up on the last day" (John 6:54). At that point, "many of his disciples drew back and no longer walked with him" (6:66).

The greater and more mysterious the love is, the more disquieting it is; paradoxically, it can push people away because it gives more and more and requires more and more. In this episode, Jesus turns to the Twelve, his closest disciples, and says, "Will you also go away?" Then Simon Peter answers him, "Lord, to whom shall we go? You have the words of eternal life; and we have believed, and have come to know, that you are the Holy One of God" (John 6:67-69).

Peter, in his relationship with the Lord, sometimes got confused, but at other times he made the deepest professions of faith. Here he remains the definitive and representative voice of the Church: "Lord, to whom shall we go?" His question presents a very pointed and penetrating look at the life of every human being and the story of all human beings. Who and what can radically save us?

This is not *a* question; it is *the* question. This outburst from Peter is so important, so dynamic and relevant, that we can relate to it very well. In many times, places, and situations, how many disappointments do we suffer as we confront life? How many dreams disappear? How many pseudo-prophets deceive us and tell us where we should go?

Peter not only posed the important question but also gave the answer: "You have the words of eternal life." All other answers are transitory and fade away; they are all in process and evolving.

Christ's words concern the eternal truth that is in God. "Eternal life" is not *a* proclamation but *the* proclamation. Life finds its fulfillment beyond the visible. Eternal life is God, who is eternal truth and eternal charity. Human beings are fulfilled when they participate in the divine.

I remember a student at the seminary, a very fine poet, who wrote a poem on the human body, which is physical but called to eternity. He described it as "our beastly divine body." His phrase highlights the unsettling paradox that is expressed throughout history. If we remain idolaters of our "I," of our ideas, of our projects, and do not convert to the "You" of God that is manifested in Christ, we will always remain incomplete, unsatisfied, and misguided. ∾

18. PREPARATIONS FOR THE FEAST OF UNLEAVENED BREAD

O n the day of the feast of Unleavened Bread in which the Passover lamb was to be sacrificed, Jesus sent Peter and John out, saying, "Go and prepare the Passover for us, that we may eat it" (Luke 22:8).

"Eating" the Passover meal is very meaningful. To eat is to transform what we eat into our own flesh and blood. This has significant value for our bodies. Jesus wanted us to accomplish the Passover event mysteriously through its assimilation on our part. In the traditional meal, the participants remembered their deliverance from slavery in Egypt; Jesus brought that symbolic meal to its fulfillment as he celebrated it by offering his body and blood as food and drink in the sacramental signs of the two elements of bread and wine.

The Passover ritual in the Old Testament was indeed symbolic. It required the preparation of many significant and profound elements. Jesus chose Peter and John to prepare the room and the other necessary items—signs that expressed the salvific work of God who had rescued his people and made then "pass over" into freedom.

John was the youngest, the virgin apostle, and Peter was the person in charge of the community of disciples, just as he would be in charge of the community of all believers. John, the virgin, is a sign of a person giving himself totally to God; virginity is an icon of a person's freedom offered as a total gift. Peter, the fisherman, is appointed to sail the ship of the Church into the waters of history and to be a "fisher of men."

Much more profoundly, "preparing the Passover," in line with the mystery of the Incarnation, means that Jesus, descending from above, took on a human body, joined it to his work, and transfigured it as his sacrament. Peter, called to do the preparation for the meal, is not the Lord of the Church but the one who "prepares" the coming of Christ, the one who also proclaims him, who opens up pathways for him, and who presents him to us.

This "diaconate" service by Peter is very important for people to gain access to the mystery of the Church. There have been quite a few perversions throughout Christian history because people have not understood, or perhaps did not want to understand, that Peter is the "preparer" of Christ's coming. Peter is the custodian of the mystery of Jesus. No one can be born without a mother; so too people cannot genuinely reach God on their own without the mediation of Jesus and, with him, of the Church that is joined to him as a bride for the regeneration of the world.

The Church has many faces, but there is only one Church. Christ came for the reconciliation of all humanity in the unity of truth and love. The vital, primary, and inescapable unity lies in the mystery of Jesus, and no one can avoid the person in charge of the Church who guards it and guides it.

The Church, because of its members, is subjected to sin and weakness, but it is under mercy. Whoever is incapable of mercy and judges the sins of others, whoever strays from the path of forgiveness, is not dwelling in the mystery of Christ. Just as there was an earlier precursor who prepared the way of the Lord (John 2:23), so too today it is Peter who points to the paths of the Lord and who prepares the feast of unity. ∾

19. "Lord, Do You Wash My Feet?"

~

Jesus and the apostles were gathered together for the Passover meal.

> Jesus, knowing that the Father had given all things into his hands, and that he had come from God and was going to God, rose from supper, laid aside his garments, and tied a towel around himself. Then he poured water into a basin, and began to wash the disciples' feet, and to wipe them with the towel that was tied around him. He came to Simon Peter; and Peter said to him, "Lord, do you wash my feet?" Jesus answered him, "What I am doing you do not know now, but afterward you will understand." Peter said to him, "You shall never wash my feet." Jesus answered him, "If I do not wash you, you have no part in me." Simon Peter said to him, "Lord, not my feet only but also my hands and my head!" (John 13:3-9)

Washing someone's feet before they sat at table was a custom among the Jews. It was typically a task for slaves to wash the feet of their masters and their guests. Jesus, who "did not count equality with God a thing to be grasped, but emptied himself, taking the form of a servant" (Philippians 2:6-7), wanted to perform the symbolic gesture of washing his disciples' feet during his last celebration of the Passover in which he instituted the Eucharist.

Peter's intuitive and spontaneous reaction is to refuse, but Jesus says that receiving this gesture signifies having a part in him. At this point, Peter accepts the mystery of the gesture, and in his own inimitable style, he replies, "Not my feet only but also my hands and my head!" (John 13:9).

What does this event tell us? Jesus is demonstrating two fundamental values: *his self- abasement* to purify human beings from pride and *our redemptive cleansing* as a result of his passion. Sin often consists in the exaltation of oneself over others; salvation comes through humility and service to others. How many jarring examples in world history are the results of pride, self-sufficiency, and climbing up the ladder over others!

Peter received the foot washing from the Lord on a human level, but he did not understand its significance; Jesus had to explain it to him. The humbling of oneself is a precondition of charity. There is no charity without profound humility. The foot washing was like an anticipation of baptism, of a passion for a continual cleansing through humility and love. When Peter realized it was not just a ritual but a redemptive action that Jesus wanted to teach and have him convey to others, he stopped protesting. In accepting that washing, he was accepting Christ the Lord, who was inaugurating a new baptism of humility that would cleanse us and redeem us through the reversal of the basic pride that is in us all.

Jesus, therefore, was anticipating in this gesture the mystery of the cross in which he would be humiliated but that would then lead to a redeemed humanity. Jesus, who would lower himself in humiliation, would then be lifted up by the Father, who would bestow on him the name that is above all other names: that Jesus Christ is Lord (Philippians 2:9, 11). ∽

20. Jesus' Farewell

ᴄᴏ

As Jesus was saying goodbye to his disciples, he told them that he was be going away to a place where they could not come.

> Simon Peter said to him, "Lord, where are you going?" Jesus answered, "Where I am going you cannot follow me now; but you shall follow afterward." Peter said to him, "Lord, why can I not follow you now? I will lay down my life for you." Jesus answered, "Will you lay down your life for me? Truly, truly, I say to you, the cock will not crow, till you have denied me three times." (John 13:36-38)

If we read the Gospels carefully, we are struck by Jesus' balanced realism. On the one hand, he set a high standard, telling his followers to imitate him and to be perfect as their heavenly Father is perfect (Matthew 5:48). On the other hand, he was always aware of the limitations in the depths of people's souls. As we see in the Gospels, Peter's enthusiasm often cooled down.

Peter, who at the time of the crucifixion would flee and hide, is sincerely asking Jesus, "Why can I not follow you now?" (John 13:37). Jesus responds by announcing to him ahead of time that because of fear and expediency, he will fail.

Enthusiasm can be emotional, but it can also be part of the ascetic life. We need to have the kind of enthusiasm that comes from this word's etymology: *en-theon*, being "in-God." This kind of enthusiasm signifies our stretching toward God, toward the other, toward the light. But we need to channel our enthusiasm well.

This very human Gospel text frames the figure of Peter, but it also reveals the vacillations of our enthusiasm. We need to remember that our human nature is subject to many moods. We all have moments of euphoria and moments of depression, and we are not usually completely in one state or the other. We need to cultivate the maturity and wisdom of heart that would lead us not to act according to what we feel but according to what we believe, hope, and love.

Character differences often incline people toward either euphoria or depression, and people should be aware of their tendencies and limitations. Above all, however, they should know how to guide their faith life according to the hope they are cultivating and the charity that inspires them.

In our spiritual lives, as we know well, there is a struggle as we make an attempt to achieve inner balance. St. Augustine's saying that we need to enter into the recesses of our inner being is very important in the spiritual life. Within us dwells the Spirit of God, which is his presence.

God expects us not to let ourselves be seduced by appearances but to govern our lives and handle our choices correctly. Our inner life should guide our emotions. Holiness, that is, union with God, is neither euphoria nor depression. It consists of accepting ourselves and letting the Spirit of God work as he permits trials and temptations to test what is in our hearts.

Having an inner life means "living together" with Christ in the Spirit, always turned toward the Father. It is helpful that John wisely says, "God is greater than our hearts" (1 John 3:20), because we are poor antennas, often closed to God's action and, at other times, open to everything else indiscriminately.

God expects us to keep a balance, but above all to guard our inner life in order to avoid becoming lifted up in our enthusiasm or depressed in our trials. God trains us to control our weaknesses and guides us with his love in all the events of life. He expects us to be listening to him at all times and not to be overwhelmed by our emotions. He trains us in a genuine faith that includes a loving awareness of Jesus' clear saying that "apart from me you can do nothing" (John 15:5). ∽

21. IN THE GARDEN OF GETHSEMANE

A fter Jesus instituted the Eucharist and he and his disciples had sung the Hallel psalms that ended the Passover supper (Psalms 113–118), they went to the Mount of Olives in Gethsemane. Gethsemane, which means "olive press," is situated in the Kedron Valley at the foot of the mount. Jesus authoritatively proclaimed his death and resurrection there when he said, "It is written, 'I will strike the shepherd, and the sheep of the flock will be scattered.' But after I am raised up, I will go before you to Galilee" (Matthew 26:31-32).

After the resurrection, the angel at the tomb made a very intriguing statement: "Tell his disciples that he has risen from the dead, and behold, he is going before you to Galilee; there you will see him" (Matthew 28:7). Jesus was setting up an appointment in Galilee, the home of the disciples. Jesus was actually saying, "You will see me resurrected in your homeland, in your own world. I will be there again, alive, the living One." And he would say to them, on that mountain in Galilee, "Behold, I am with you always, to the close of the age" (Matthew 28:20).

In the Garden of Gethsemane, Jesus says, "Watch and pray that you may not enter into temptation; the spirit indeed is willing, but the flesh is weak" (Matthew 26:41). When he finds Peter and the others asleep, he says to Peter, "So, could you not watch with me one hour?" (26:40). Jesus finds them asleep a second time, and the third time he says, "Are you still sleeping and taking your rest? Behold, the hour is at hand, and the Son of man is betrayed into the hands of sinners" (26:45).

At the time of his passion, Jesus was in profound travail at prayer as he contemplated his sacrifice for all human beings that would accomplish the salvation willed by his Father. But he found the disciples absent, asleep, basically avoiding the situation.

The Lord knows our changeable condition and our weakness. He only asks that we have a sincere heart. Paul, with impressive realism, affirms—and so should we all— that "if I must boast, I will boast of the things that show my weakness" (2 Corinthians 11:30). He adds, "To keep me from being too elated by the abundance of revelations, a thorn was given me in the flesh, a messenger of Satan" (12:7). Because of this, he asks the Lord three times to remove it, but the Lord says, "My grace is sufficient for you, for my power is made perfect in weakness" (12:9).

Paul also says—and this could exactly describe Peter's emotional behavior—"I will all the more gladly boast of my weaknesses, that the power of Christ may rest upon me. For the sake of Christ, then, I am content with weaknesses, insults, hardships, persecutions, and calamities; for when I am weak, then I am strong" (2 Corinthians 12:9-10).

The Lord does not condemn us for our weaknesses. In fact, he can reveal his glory through them. ∽

22. FOLLOWING AT A DISTANCE

∾

Outward appearance, possessing a certain status, and being well dressed mean nothing to the Lord. Our faith and our hearts are what count. Judas, one of the Twelve, is a bitter symbol of the worship of money. Jesus taught, "No one can serve two masters; for either he will hate the one and love the other, or he will be devoted to the one and despise the other. You cannot serve God and mammon" (Matthew 6:24).

People say that money can be the best servant, but it is always the worst master. It can make people such slaves that they will sacrifice their honor and their way of life to defend their treasure, and actions that are generally considered loving are turned upside down and become evil. Judas sullied his friendship with Jesus through his betrayal with a kiss that was not a sign of love but, in this case, a sign of wickedness: "The one I shall kiss is the man; seize him" (Matthew 26:48).

Jesus is recognized by that predetermined signal and arrested. One of those who are with him draws his sword and strikes the servant of the high priest and cuts off his ear. Jesus reproves him, saying, "Put your sword back into its place; for all who take the sword will perish by the sword" (Matthew 26:52).

Peter "followed him at a distance . . . , and going inside he sat with the guards to see the end" (Matthew 26:58). Peter is a terrified but faithful follower. Fear has many causes, but it is ultimately the sign of weak faith and immature love. To follow at a distance is to be an observer and not to be alongside someone. However, there is in Peter's attitude a tenderness that is moving. He is the only one who accompanies Jesus at the beginning of his passion, even though it is at a distance.

Following Christ does not mean looking at him from afar. In our experience as weak believers, we demonstrate so many different ways of pseudo-following. We are followers of Jesus because of tradition, or culture, or fear. We are not always followers because we have surrendered our lives to him. Protecting ourselves is a widespread tactic that leads us to betray him—the very one who does not destroy our "I" but transforms it. Our disguises are tactics that lead us away from simplicity of heart and into blind alleys.

Paul exhorts the Corinthians to have "genuine love" (2 Corinthians 6:6). Peter will have such an experience in the light of the resurrection and in the power of the Holy Spirit, who will descend upon him and the other apostles. Only through the sublime dimension of the power of God do we overcome our state of impotence.

Jesus tells us, "Apart from me you can do nothing" (John 15:5). Only through vital communion with him will we be strong in the way the prophet Jeremiah describes: "And I, behold, I make you this day a fortified city, an iron pillar, and bronze walls, against the whole land, against the kings of Judah, its princes, its priests, and the people of the land. They will fight against you; but they shall not prevail against you, for I am with you, says the LORD, to deliver you" (1:18-19).

Peter is our brother in his weakness, but he is our father and model when the Spirit of God transforms him. On the day of Pentecost, Peter will loudly proclaim the power of God working in people's hearts as he quotes the prophet Joel:

I will pour out my Spirit upon all flesh,
and your sons and your daughters shall prophesy,
and your young men shall see visions,
and your old men shall dream dreams;
yes, and on my menservants and my maidservants in
those days
I will pour out my Spirit; and they shall prophesy.
(Acts 2:17-18)

And it will be the case that on that day, "whoever calls on the name of the Lord shall be saved" (Acts 2:21). ∾

23. PETER'S DENIAL

ᔭ

Jesus had told Peter in the Garden of Gethsemane, "Truly, I say to you, this very night, before the cock crows, you will deny me three times" (Matthew 26:34). Peter spontaneously and emotionally responded, "Even if I must die with you, I will not deny you" (26:35). Jesus' prediction of Peter's betrayal came from his awareness of Peter's weakness. In the context of the paschal mystery—the mystery for all human beings and for all time—a frightened Peter will deny him three times, just as Jesus had predicted.

We meet Peter's heart again as he follows at a distance, when he is the only disciple still following Jesus. He is, in the end, obstinately faithful, even if his actions are confused. Peter moves us; his solitary state here foreshadows the many trials and bitter disappointments of his successors as they govern the Church.

Now Peter was sitting outside in the courtyard. And a maid came up to him, and said, "You also were with Jesus the Galilean." But he denied it before them all, saying, "I do not know what you mean." And when he went out to the porch, another maid saw him, and she said to the bystanders, "This man was with Jesus of Nazareth." And again he denied it with an oath, "I do not know the man." After a little while the bystanders came up and said to Peter, "Certainly you are also one of them, for your accent betrays you." Then he began to invoke a curse on himself and to swear, "I do not know the man." And immediately the cock crowed. And Peter remembered the saying of Jesus, "Before the cock crows, you will deny me three times." And he went out and wept bitterly. (Matthew 26:69-75)

This episode in Peter's life and in salvation history is very intense emotionally. It reveals both the heart of a man and the mysterious working of God. It offers at least four points for reflection: the female perspective of the Praetorian's servants; the clear denials by Peter, who was alone, loving but humanly defeated; the crowing of the rooster, which made him recall the Lord's prediction; and his bitter weeping over his spiritual defeat.

Peter sits down outside the courtyard. Whoever is not standing on his feet is not staying alert. Two maidservants appear, and finally some in the group recognize him as a disciple of Jesus. They had seen Peter before with his master, and he is still with his master but at a distance, suffering the drama of his master's trial. Fear and confusion put him on the defensive.

When we are in fear, our first defense is often a lie. It is the reversal of the dynamic of communication and testimony to truth and charity. Peter hides behind a hastily convenient answer: "I don't know who he is; I don't know him." He protects himself by distancing himself from Jesus. This will not be the case when the risen Lord appears to him and the Spirit enlightens him. As Paul tells the Galatians, "The fruit of the Spirit is . . . faithfulness" (5:22).

It is certain, however, that every lie is a betrayal of God who is the truth. It is also true that fear is still, at bottom, the worship of self, thus reflecting the difficulty of presenting oneself to the light, since "the Spirit is the truth" (1 John 5:7). It is striking that when a person presumes to remove Christ from the picture, pettiness, gossip, and an interest in others' errors emerge. The Gospel tells us that in defending his betrayal, Peter invoked a curse upon himself and swore. The strength behind a lie does not usually come from peace and calmness.

The voice of God is nevertheless always present. The deeper the abyss, the more one yearns for the light. The rooster was announcing the approaching dawn, but in Peter's case, it was the fulfillment of Jesus' words: "Before the cock crows, you will deny me three times" (Matthew 26:75).

Peter's denials were not ideological but situational. The temptation to deny the Lord can be an unforeseen occasion or a daily continual habit. Peter became dismayed and terrified, so he decisively stated, "I do not know the man" (Matthew 26:72). He was an onlooker in line with his psychology. He was not a shrewd, calculating man but an emotional, weak man.

Paradoxically, I must say that although he drew back, he did not stop loving. He withdrew and fled, but Jesus was in his heart. He will come back out when the storm has passed. Peter is not a model of betrayal but of confusion, and his generous, enthusiastic personality will burst forth when the Spirit fills him.

Later, Jesus will ask for an answer concerning his love: "Do you love me?" (John 21:16). Every betrayal, every deceitfulness of heart, finds its redemption in love. Peter's bitter weeping is already the beginning of salvation as an inner washing. Given our inherent weakness and propensity for falling, we are saved by the power of Christ's love but also by our repentance.

The Lord knows our hearts and our weakness, but he always prepares us. Peter, in his denials, is a representative figure of the

Church, which is holy but must always purify itself. To be a Christian does not entail Promethean perfection but facing who we are and saying to the Lord, "Have mercy on me, a sinner." ∽

24. PETER'S ABSENCE AT THE CROSS

ও

John concludes his narration of Jesus' crucifixion in this way:
"They shall look on him whom they have pierced" (19:37).
Isaiah had prophesied, "He had no form or comeliness that
we should look at him, / and no beauty that we should desire
him" (53:2).

Peter did not want to be at the crucifixion. Of the Twelve, only
John was present. Judas had killed himself in despair over his
betrayal of Jesus: "This man bought a field with the reward of
his wickedness; and falling headlong he burst open in the middle
and all his bowels gushed out" (Acts 1:18). The other ten disciples, including Peter, stayed away out of fear.

What does Peter's absence at Jesus' crucifixion mean? We need
to begin with the point that crucifixion was not an event that
people generally attended. Jesus' crucifixion, however, is the linch-
pin of our faith and the precursor to the resurrection. Without a
strong faith, people flee from the cross and become bewildered.
Several times Jesus had said to the disciples, "Have you no faith?"
(Mark 4:40; cf. Luke 825; cf. Matthew 8:26). He linked their lack
of faith not only to their failure to surrender their whole lives but
also to fear.

Peter was the first apostle to witness the resurrection and the
first great preacher of the paschal mystery of Jesus. When the Holy
Spirit came down, the mystery of the crucified and risen Jesus was
revealed to his heart. He preached it to everyone. He saw it as the
meaning of existence. He will later write in his first letter, "Rejoice
in so far as you share Christ's sufferings, that you may also rejoice

and be glad when his glory is revealed" (1 Peter 4:13). He himself was crucified for Christ and chose to be crucified upside down, so there is a mysterious redemption in his life.

But can Peter's absence at Jesus' crucifixion be in any way considered as a type of presence? To be present to God as he is to us is not easy; it is the fruit of a deep, ongoing conversion. We ordinarily are absent from God, but our absences are not always meant to exclude God. They are signs of our weakness and immaturity.

It seems to me that Peter's absence at the cross, other than revealing fear, reveals the degree of his assimilation of the mystery of Jesus. Every life comes from an embryo; so too faith is embryonic and develops gradually, even to the point of preparing a person for martyrdom.

In a mysterious way, certain absences from God are in themselves crucifying. There are absences in which the truth of his presence begins to develop. Peter shows himself humanly weak, but he is the one who, in line with his temperament, shows periods of growth along with weakness in his choices. He always comes across as a frank and honest man who is not in the least bit hypocritical.

Jesus plants the seed of holiness, of martyrdom, in Peter's heart, and that already indicates the mystery of the Church that is simultaneously divine and human, holy and sinful. Peter, even in his physical absence from the crucifixion, teaches us about the hard work involved in the journey of every sincere soul.

God has many ways of being present to people, but people have only one way of being present to him: to open up to him, even if the process is gradual and requires effort. ∾

25. THE EMPTY TOMB

Now on the first day of the week, Mary Magdalene came to the tomb early, while it was still dark, and saw that the stone had been taken away from the tomb. So she ran, and went to Simon Peter and the other disciple, the one whom Jesus loved, and said to them, "They have taken the Lord out of the tomb, and we do not know where they have laid him." Peter then came out with the other disciple, and they went toward the tomb. They both ran, but the other disciple outran Peter and reached the tomb first; and stooping to look in, he saw the linen cloths lying there, but he did not go in. Then Simon Peter came, following him, and went into the tomb; he saw the linen cloths lying, and the napkin, which had been on his head, not lying with the linen cloths but rolled up in a place by itself. Then the other disciple, who reached the tomb first, also went in, and he saw and believed; for as yet they did not know the Scripture, that he must rise from the dead. Then the disciples went back to their homes. (John 20:1-10)

The day after the Sabbath is the day of the Lord's resurrection, of our resurrection. *Surrexit Dominus vere, alleluia*! The Lord is risen indeed, alleluia!

It is still dark. But one woman's heart is alert and awake. Mary Magdalene had met Jesus, and he had changed her life. He had given her existence meaning and brought joy to her heart. She braves the night by herself with a determined heart. She goes to the tomb and finds that the rock sealing the tomb has been rolled aside. Jesus is not there—or better, he had been there but cannot be found there any more.

She is the first witness of the new creation. The woman who was already born anew because of Jesus is the first one to see the greatest sign in history by which people live and have hope: victory over death. St. Paul cries out, "O death, where is your victory?" (1 Corinthians 15:55). This woman, although profoundly affected, does not become confused. She had learned from Jesus' teaching that she had a home where she could find him: the Church, which Peter had been assigned to guide and whose unity he was to maintain. Because of that, she runs to Peter and John, the two emblematic disciples. Peter, the head, was its guardian; John was the sign of its heart, of the love she sought and contemplated. She is not hysterically excited but realistic. Jesus' buried body is no longer there; he is no longer walled in and closed off. And she hazards a very human hypothesis: they have taken his body elsewhere, but we do not know where.

Peter and John are informed of the facts, and they listen to what she says. He is not in the tomb, but where is he? The two disciples run to the tomb. The news is mind-boggling.

John's youth enables him to run faster. He arrives first but does not enter first. That gesture is not merely a sign of good manners toward one's elders, but a sign of respect toward Peter, the one in charge of building the Church, the rock for that building, its leader, its guide.

Peter is the first to enter the tomb that has become the place not of definitive death but of risen life forever and for all humanity. John records the episode in his Gospel and humbly omits his name, using the generic name of "the other disciple" (20:3). Although he does not give his name, he tells us that in that place, at that empty tomb, "he saw and believed" (20:8). To see! What a powerful and significant statement!

At the beginning of Jesus' earthly life, Simeon, an elderly devout man praying in the Temple, held the baby who was the expectation of all history and said, "My eyes have seen your salvation" (Luke 2:30). Here instead, a young man, very moved, confesses, "I went in; I saw and believed."

Faith is not an adventure that occurs in the dark; it does not work against reason. Faith is the experience of becoming aware that God cannot remain in the places of death. John writes, "In him was life, and the life was the light of men" (1:4).

The two disciples did not initially grasp the greatness, the power, and the light of the resurrection event. God does not overwhelm us; he leads us according to our ability to receive and respond. Faith, then, has a maturation time, and faith gradually comes to understand that Jesus *must* be raised from the dead. John, one of the first witnesses of the resurrection, highlights this: "For as yet they did not know the Scripture, that he must rise from the dead" (20:9).

Peter and John return home, but they would now go out into the world. History would become their home. Every person has a vocation that comes at a certain time. This episode points to the primacy of Peter but also to the need for faith to mature in each of us, no matter who we are.

Today and always, it is fitting to look at the first witness and the great laywoman Mary Magdalene, and to grasp with her that Jesus' tomb is empty and that he is at the center of history, risen and always dynamically alive. ∽

26. LEAPING INTO THE SEA

The episode I propose for this meditation is the epilogue from John's Gospel that was added either by John or one of his disciples. It deals with one of the post-resurrection appearances of Jesus: "Jesus revealed himself again to the disciples by the Sea of Tiberias" (John 21:1).

John notes that Simon Peter, Thomas, Nathanael of Cana, the sons of Zebedee, and two other disciples are together (21:2). One of the main protagonists in this post-resurrection appearance is, of course, Peter. He tells the others he is going fishing, and the others decide to go with him. "They went out and got into the boat; but that night they caught nothing" (21:3). At dawn after fruitless labor, Jesus appears on the shore, but the disciples do not recognize him.

It often happens that Jesus walks alongside us, that he is involved in certain circumstances of our lives, but we are not aware of it. We are distracted by our own thoughts and caught up in our own worries, and so we do not function with the "eyes of faith" and are not able to see that the Lord is with us.

Jesus asks the disciples who do not recognize him, "Children, have you any fish?" (John 21:5). Jesus' approach is very human. Meeting people in his name means meeting them in their lives, in their trials, in their expectations, in their needs. Since the disciples have, in fact, caught nothing, they answer, "No."

Jesus then tells them, "Cast the net on the right side of the boat, and you will find some" (John 21:6). A fisherman who was one of my parishioners in a coastal city explained to me that ordinarily, nets are not cast on the right. This shows that God is not bound by human ways of doing things; he surpasses them and often turns them upside down. The catch is miraculous: they cannot pull up the nets because of the abundance of fish.

John, the "disciple whom Jesus loved" (what a wonderful phrase to express a relationship with Jesus!), tells Peter, "It is the Lord!" (John 21:7). Knowing when to say this in the trials of life, in the good and bad times, is very comforting and illuminating. "It is the Lord"—the One who has the key to every heart and to all of history.

Peter, contrary to the norm in such a case, does not remain naked before he jumps into the water; instead, he puts on a tunic. His direct spontaneity shows through again. The others, though, are pulling up the nets full of fish. Arriving on the beach, they see a charcoal fire with fish and bread being cooked. The Gospel says, "Jesus said to them, 'Bring some of the fish that you have just caught.' So Simon Peter went aboard and hauled the net ashore, full of large fish . . . ; and although there were so many, the net was not torn" (John 21:10-11).

I believe that the fresh fish from the catch is symbolic of "our daily bread." This phrase from Jesus' teaching—"Give us each day our daily bread" (Luke 11:3)—means we should not worry about what we will eat because the Father, as they say back home, "sees and provides."

When the Lord appears here, he is not recognized. Instead, he reveals himself as a mysterious presence that the text describes this way: "Now none of the disciples dared ask him, 'Who are you?' They knew it was the Lord" (John 21:12). The disciples were astounded but not confused.

To be overwhelmed by the presence of the Lord means that no questions are asked; there is only an adoring, contemplative silence. In this third time after the resurrection that Jesus appeared to his disciples, he appeared in a way that evoked the Eucharist. The text says, "Jesus came and took the bread and gave it to them, and so with the fish" (John 21:13). ❧

27. "DO YOU LOVE ME MORE THAN THESE?"

A fter eating fish from the miraculous catch with his disciples, Jesus focused on Peter. It is very important for our faith and for the Church to look at the dialogue and especially Jesus' definitive statements.

> When they had finished breakfast, Jesus said to Simon Peter, "Simon, son of John, do you love me more than these?" He said to him, "Yes, Lord; you know that I love you." He said to him, "Feed my lambs." A second time he said to him, "Simon, son of John, do you love me?" He said to him, "Yes, Lord; you know that I love you." He said to him, "Tend my sheep." He said to him the third time, "Simon, son of John, do you love me?" Peter was grieved because he said to him the third time, "Do you love me?" And he said to him, "Lord, you know everything; you know that I love you." Jesus said to him, "Feed my sheep. Truly, truly, I say to you, when you were young, you fastened your own belt and walked where you would; but when you are old, you will stretch out your hands, and another will fasten your belt for you and carry you where you do not wish to go." (This he said to show by what death he was to glorify God.) And after this he said to him, "Follow me." (John 21:15-19)

Three times Jesus asks Peter, who will pastor the Church, if he loves him. In the first instance, Jesus asks Peter if he loves him "more than these" (John 21:15). To be a pastor in the Church and, in Peter's case, a pastor of the whole Church, requires intense love. To look after the Church requires love. One can see a reference to Peter's triple denial in Jesus' triple question about faithful love.

Peter's threefold profession of devotion to Jesus corresponds to a triple investiture: Jesus entrusted Peter with the care of overseeing the flock in his name (Matthew 16:18). It could be that a threefold repetition was a sign of a commitment, a contract, a required format according to Semitic custom. What is certain, though, is that Jesus insistently asks the question, and that in itself is significant. It is a very intense conversation. Peter repeats, "You know that I love you" (John 21:15, 16, 17), which could mean, "I have already proved it" or, more likely, "You have searched me and you know me." This moment in Peter's life was of great importance for him and for the Church, and it was conducted with very moving tenderness.

Jesus asks for Peter's love and prophesies his martyrdom. In this very important context, Jesus tells him conclusively, "Follow me" (John 21:19). This phrase sheds light on the "feeding of the flock," because following Jesus is at the heart of the pastor's mission.

In the conclusion to John's Gospel, there is an episode that is worth analyzing and contemplating. After Jesus tells Peter to follow him, John, who in this case is also a participant in the scene, tells us, "Peter turned and saw following them the disciple whom Jesus loved, who had lain close to his breast at the supper. . . . When Peter saw him, he said to Jesus, 'Lord, what about this man?' Jesus said to him, 'If it is my will that he remain until I come, what is that to you? Follow me'" (John 21:20-22). Because of this exchange, the rumor among some people about the disciple John was that he would not die. However, John is quite specific: "Jesus did not say to him that he was not to die, but, 'If it is my will that he remain until I come, what is that to you?'" (21:23).

It seems to me that the two great apostles were not really being contrasted; they were each trying to understand his mystery, his future, based on what the Lord had said. They were both passionate about Jesus—Peter, with his instant exuberance, and John, with his contemplative approach. The Gospel of John ultimately ends by teaching us that it is up to every one of us to follow Jesus. What will happen later, even martyrdom, is mysteriously also a vocation.

Peter died a martyr in Rome, and John was imprisoned on the island of Patmos for the testimony of his faith (Revelation 1:9). In John's vision there, Jesus laid his hand on him and said, "Fear not, I am the first and the last, and the living one; I died, and behold I am alive for evermore, and I have the keys of Death and Hades" (Revelation 1:17-18). It is John, the virgin Evangelist, who emphasizes the coming of Christ rather than his glory, and Revelation ends on that note: "He who testifies to these things says, 'Surely I am coming soon.' Amen. Come, Lord Jesus!" (22:20). ❧

28. THE COMPANY OF APOSTLES

A fter Jesus' ascension into heaven, the apostles returned to Jerusalem. The Acts of the Apostles says this:

> They went up to the upper room, where they were staying, Peter and John and James and Andrew, Philip and Thomas, Bartholomew and Matthew, James the son of Alphaeus and Simon the Zealot and Judas the son of James. All these with one accord devoted themselves to prayer, together with the women and Mary the mother of Jesus, and with his brethren. (Acts 1:13-14)

This text, which seems merely descriptive, is actually quite full of meaning. It reveals the face of the Church at its beginning. It emphasizes that for the first time after the Ascension but before Pentecost, the Church demonstrated and lived out "being together." They already had a place to meet. There were only eleven apostles now. Judas, who had committed suicide, was of course missing.

It is striking that the author of Acts does not list the apostles singly but lists them two by two. Furthermore, he does so without considering the biological ties that exist. For example, he does not list Peter and Andrew together, who are brothers, but Peter and John. He does not link James and John, who are brothers, but James and Andrew. This group is, in fact, a group that was born from above: the apostles. As the text notes, "With one accord [they] devoted themselves to prayer" (Acts 1:14).

What is also noteworthy is that the apostles do not gather together in an elitist fashion. They accept some women, especially Mary, along with some of Jesus' relatives, into their radical prayer community.

Mary, the mother of Jesus, is effectively both a mother *in* the Church and *of* the Church. After Jesus' crucifixion, Mary disappears in the Gospel texts, but she now appears in a new dimension of spiritual motherhood. The mother of Christ and of those who believe in him is, through the mystery of universal redemption, the mother of the whole human race. She is, the text says, with Jesus' relatives. The word "brother" [brethren] in the Bible also means a close or distant relative, but beyond that, this word also indicates that the first community of believers involved a fellowship of sharing in the new life of the Spirit.

Believers, children of the same Father, are brothers and sisters in the love that is God. Peter in his first letter will say, "Having purified your souls by your obedience to the truth for a sincere love of the brethren, love one another earnestly from the heart. You have been born anew, not of perishable seed but of imperishable, through the living and abiding word of God" (1 Peter 1:22-23). ∽

29. JUDAS' REPLACEMENT

eter stood up in the midst of the brethren and said that Judas "was numbered among us, and was allotted his share in this ministry" (Acts 1:17). Acts also records his tragic ending when he was destroyed by remorse (1:18). Peter then declares, "One of the men who have accompanied us during all the time that the Lord Jesus went in and out among us, beginning from the baptism of John until the day when he was taken up from us—one of these men must become with us a witness to his resurrection" (1:21-22). Two individuals were put forth: Joseph, called Barsabbas, and Matthias. "And they cast lots for them, and the lot fell on Matthias; and he was enrolled with the eleven apostles" (1:26).

There needed to be twelve apostles because there were twelve tribes of Israel. Israel was a foreshadowing of the new people of God that was born from Jesus' mission and paschal mystery. For that reason, Peter decided someone needed to be chosen to take Judas' place. This is how the apostolic college reconstitutes itself. This is an expression of episcopal collegiality related to apostolic collegiality that would always remain in the Church in its originality and uniqueness. The one who provided for the constitutive integrity as well as for the organization of the life of the Church was Peter. Peter was the head of the apostolic college. He was also the guide for the Church and remains so forever though his successors.

The Church has a visible face, a hierarchical organization, as Christ willed. The methods of choosing successors may change, but no one can decide by himself to put himself forward as a guide. In Christ's Church, the first guarantor is Peter. Members of the community need to be heard and consulted, but theirs is not the definitive voice. The Church comes from above, and it has a hierarchical structure.

The choice of Judas' successor to the apostolic college was not made based on any cultural norms or organizational ability. It was based on his being a witness, together with the others, of the resurrection of Jesus. As we read the New Testament Scriptures, it is clear that proclaiming and testifying to the resurrection of Jesus is the primary mission in the life of an apostle. Jesus' resurrection is the light, the power, the hope of the Church, so much so that "if Christ has not been raised, your faith is futile and you are still in your sins" (I Corinthians 15:17).

The crucified One is not a defeated Christ but the One who freely offered himself for us and for the whole human race. Now risen, he is forever alive and is the Lord of history.

The Church will always be alive because it lives in Christ, who is the same yesterday, today, and forever (cf. Hebrews 13:8). Christians should never be distraught like the people who do not have the hope that flows from Easter. No human power can conquer death. Only Jesus can say, "Fear not, I am the first and the last, and the living one; I died, and behold I am alive for evermore, and I have the keys of Death and Hades" (Revelation 1:17-18). ∞

30. Peter's First Sermon

Peter's first sermon after Pentecost is a masterpiece of faith, wisdom, and rhetoric. The Holy Spirit had come down. Universal reconciliation was occurring as "each one heard them speaking in his own language" (Acts 2:6). All were surprised: "All were amazed and perplexed, saying to one another, 'What does this mean?' But others mocking said, 'They are filled with new wine'" (2:12-13). In the face of mystery, reason, which claims to be our only means of understanding, can misunderstand the situation.

Peter stands up, and together with the other eleven, speaks out loudly. When he gets the attention of the crowd, he says,

These men are not drunk, as you suppose, since it is only the third hour of the day; but this is what was spoken by the prophet Joel:
And in the last days it shall be, God declares, that I will pour out my Spirit upon all flesh, and your sons and your daughters shall prophesy, and your young men shall see visions, and your old men shall dream dreams. (Acts 2:15-17)

Peter then announces the *kerygma*: "God raised him up, having loosed the pangs of death, because it was not possible for him to be held by it" (Acts 2:24). He goes on to say, "This Jesus God raised up, and of that we are all witnesses. Being therefore exalted at the right hand of God, and having received from the Father the promise of the Holy Spirit, he has poured out this which you see and hear" (2:32-33).

Peter ends his proclamation by saying, "Let all the house of Israel therefore know assuredly that God has made him both Lord and Christ, this Jesus whom you crucified" (Acts 2:36). When the people ask how they should respond, Peter tells them, "Repent, and be baptized every one of you in the name of Jesus Christ for the forgiveness of your sins; and you shall receive the gift of the Holy Spirit" (2:38).

Peter becomes the interpreter of God's works. He explains them with biblical references, making clear that this event is what people have been awaiting from God. The gift of the Spirit—an event that renews human beings, their lives on earth, and their hope—receives its profound and practical explanation through Peter. He demonstrates the working of God in human beings and calls people to conversion.

Peter's sermon demonstrates that authentic preaching has two vital components that help us avoid falling into trivialities and mere conceptualizations. The first is to announce and demonstrate the work of God, and the second is to offer people help in accepting that work into their lives.

The acceptance of Christ, who is our salvation, is shown through the conversion of hearts. I truly believe that all our preaching, all our pastoral duty, despite new times, new circumstances, and new vocabulary, cannot avoid the *kerygma*. It is the proclamation of salvation and shows how much the Lord has done and is still doing for us. Without this proclamation, it is easy to fall back into presenting intellectual and conceptual frameworks that do not save.

Peter was acting in his role as the guardian of God's work. Peter explained the word of God and his saving action, and once the people heard what he said, they received it, and in receiving it, they were saved. ∾

31. THE FIRST CONVERTS

ᴄ⌍

In his sermon to the crowd at Pentecost, Peter clearly and force-fully proclaimed the mystery of Jesus, and the reaction of the people was immediate. When they heard what Peter said,

> They were cut to the heart, and said to Peter, "Brethren, what shall we do?" And Peter said to them, "Repent, and be baptized every one of you in the name of Jesus Christ for the forgiveness of your sins; and you shall receive the gift of the Holy Spirit. For the promise is to you and to your children and to all that are far off, every one whom the Lord our God calls to him." And he testified with many other words and exhorted them, saying, "Save yourselves from this crooked generation." (Acts 2:37-40)

When the people responded to Peter's preaching, "those who received his word were baptized, and there were added that day about three thousand souls" (Acts 2:41).

Peter, the fisherman who was now a fisher of men because of the mission entrusted to him by the Lord Jesus, is the one to address the crowds at Pentecost. He emphasizes the mystery of Christ, asserting that the Father has made Jesus Lord. In order to open their hearts to conversion, he reminds the people that they crucified Jesus. What a chastisement! His preaching does not coddle the crowd; it is not aimed at their mental assent but at the conversion of their hearts.

Christ's presence on the cross pronounces a judgment on the world. On that cross we see not only God's unspeakable love but also all our wickedness, our lack of attention to God, and perhaps our attempt to remove him from our lives so that we can move ahead with our own plans and dreams.

Peter touches the people in their depths: "They were cut to the heart" (Acts 2:37). Preaching is not an intellectual activity that touches the mind; it is meant to lead instead to conversion. The text says the hearers asked, "Brethren, what shall we do?" (2:37). Note that they have begun to call the apostles "brethren." This is already a sign of God working and of their conversion.

Peter calls for repentance and baptism in the name of Jesus for the remission of sin and tells them that they will receive the gift of the Holy Spirit and the fulfillment of God's promises. He ends on a practical note by exhorting them to save themselves from the current perverse generation.

Peter lays out a specific sequence that links God's action in their lives to the opening of their hearts and their choices. This is the paradigmatic sequence in preaching for every community and for all believers: purify people's faith, and then explain how to make it specific by translating it into their lives.

Today we speak, and rightly so, of "pastoral plans," and that can be an inspired approach, provided that we emphasize the revelation of Christ the Savior in our projects and in the methods we use. In other words, we need to return to the *kerygma*. When the food is good, everyone comes for it. There is a great need today for a re-presentation of Christ—not a vague, intellectual, or moralistic presentation, but a vital and essential re-presentation that opens up paths to faith.

Truth draws people. The fruit of Peter's catechesis was the baptism of three thousand people, according to Acts. The pulpit for Peter's proclamation was not inside the Temple but in the courtyard square. Evangelization does not mean trying to gather a congregation; it means speaking to people where they are. We need to leave the Temple so that we can return to the Temple with others.

Peter presented the first straightforward, powerful, and animated evangelization. He proved to be a guide for believers and an evangelist for nonbelievers. As such, he is the model for all times and places. ∽

32. HEALING THE LAME BEGGAR

~

One day Peter and John went up to the Temple around 3:00 p.m. to pray (Acts 3:1). The Church lives, breathes, and functions when it is a community that prays. Prayer is the personal and communal opening of ourselves to God through which we sense his presence and his response to us. The early Church teaches us this example.

As we can still observe in many places today, the poor are attracted to the house of God. They sense that it is their home. People seek fellowship in God's house; they succeed in overcoming their state of aloneness in that place. And this is precisely what we see in the Acts of the Apostles: "A man lame from birth was being carried, whom they laid daily at that gate of the temple which is called Beautiful to ask alms of those who entered the temple" (Acts 3:2).

This man probably did not know who Peter and John were when he was begging alms from them. When they entered the Temple, Peter looked at him and along with John said, "Look at us" (Acts 3:4). We first need to show our faces, our hearts, to the poor. Peter's phrase is paradigmatic: "Look at us." It means that before giving something, we give ourselves, our hearts. The lame man, bewildered by Peter's saying, was expecting some kind of alms. However, Peter said to him, "I have no silver and gold, but I give you what I have; in the name of Jesus Christ of Nazareth, rise and walk" (3:6).

This declaration by Peter, the first pontiff of the Church, is significant. He declares that although he has no money, he is a mediator of the power of God and can therefore tell a lame man, "In the name of Jesus Christ of Nazareth, rise and walk." The power of the Church is the power of God that deals with the frailty of human beings. It does not lie in material goods; material goods are useful, but they are never the goal.

Peter "took him by the right hand and raised him up; and immediately his feet and ankles were made strong" (Acts 3:7). The power of God can also be expressed through our arms but above all through our hearts.

The lame man was invigorated, and "leaping up he stood and walked and entered the temple with them, walking and leaping and praising God" (Acts 3:8). The three verbs in this sacred text need to be highlighted because they indicate the effects of the power of God that came through Peter and John: "walking," "leaping," and "praising" God. Every miracle is one of God's marvelous deeds, and like every divine action, it produces exaltation and joy. God is joy; he is optimism. Sometimes God is seen as an obstacle to people's self-affirmation, but that reverses the truth: the power of God makes the lame man walk.

Peter, John, and the beggar enter the Temple and praise God, causing "wonder and amazement" (Acts 3:10). The lame man who is now walking clings to Peter and John (3:11). He had been isolated before when he was begging; now he is walking with the apostles. He had needed to make himself noticed before; now the people are following him. The development of human beings does not occur through having possessions or power; it occurs in social and interpersonal relationships in which those who cannot walk are helped to walk.

Peter, seeing this, asks the people, "Men of Israel, why do you wonder at this, or why do you stare at us, as though by our own power or piety we had made him walk?" (Acts 3:12). How wonderful for Peter to unite the power that comes from God to a spirituality that looks at others the way God wants us to! A person who shows mercy becomes a channel for the power of God.

Peter, who belonged to the crucified One, now announces him again as the risen One, and he will do so continuously and convincingly in the future. In this situation, he tells the people that they "killed the Author of life, whom God raised from the dead. To this we are witnesses. And his name, by faith in his name, has made this man strong whom you see and know; and the faith which is through Jesus has given the man this perfect health in the presence of you all" (Acts 3:15-16).

Faith is the power of God in the midst of our lack of power. Peter saw other "lame" people before him, the ones who closed themselves up in the face of Jesus and did not have hearts to welcome him or feet to follow him. Peter recognized their recalcitrance and exhorted them to repent and change their lives so "that your sins may be blotted out, that times of refreshing may come from the presence of the Lord" (Acts 3:19).

Jesus had earlier said to a lame man, "For which is easier, to say, 'Your sins are forgiven,' or to say, 'Rise and walk'?" (Matthew 9:5). He gave the paralytic the ability to walk in order to affirm his redemption from the greater paralysis of being left in his sins. A powerful point for meditation is presented here: without the salvific work and power of God in Jesus, we remain in our sins, and as a consequence, we are paralyzed on the path of our lives. ✑

33. Peter and John before the Sanhedrin

പ

In chapter 4 of Acts, several faces of the true Church of Christ appear: it is a holy, catholic, apostolic Church, but also a persecuted Church. In the text we will examine, a very serious question is put forth for our contemplation.

When the whole Christian community sees the persecution of Peter and John, they turn to God and pray:

> "Sovereign Lord, who made the heaven and the earth and the sea and everything in them, who by the mouth of our father David, your servant, said by the Holy Spirit,
>
> > 'Why did the Gentiles rage,
> > and the peoples imagine vain things?
> > The kings of the earth set themselves in array,
> > and the rulers were gathered together,
> > against the Lord and against his Anointed'—
>
> for truly in this city there were gathered together against your holy servant Jesus, whom you anointed, both Herod and Pontius Pilate, with the Gentiles and the peoples of Israel." (Acts 4:24-27)

The early Church, along with Peter, found itself in the mystery of the cross that was being perpetuated. Why does persecution happen? It comes from the perennial conflict between human pride and independence and the truth and humility of Christ and of his genuine followers.

Peter, who at times had been confused prior to the descent of the Spirit, clearly and forcefully continues to proclaim the cross of Christ and his resurrection, this time to the Sanhedrin. He speaks boldly, saying,

> "Rulers of the people and elders, if we are being examined today concerning a good deed done to a cripple, by what means this man has been healed, be it known to you all, and to all the people of Israel, that by the name of Jesus Christ of Nazareth, whom you crucified, whom God raised from the dead, by him this man is standing before you well. This is the stone which was rejected by you builders, but which has become the cornerstone. And there is salvation in no one else, for there is no other name under heaven given among men by which we must be saved." (Acts 4:8-12)

Peter's forcefulness, frankness, and faith contrast in a glaring way with the mean-spirited, faithless, and hostile attitude of the persecutors. When people speak out of polemic opposition rather than from the basis of a truth, they appear petty and confused. The truth is straightforward. People who set themselves against it are like people who put on blinders and then say the sun does not exist.

It is interesting to see the Sanhedrin's bewilderment and uncertainty in the question they ask themselves: "What shall we do with these men? For that a notable sign has been performed through them is manifest" (Acts 4:16). They speak of a "notable sign" but wriggle away from its effect, from the significance of the event, taking refuge in the typical subterfuge of people who are unwilling to believe. They conclude, "But in order that it may spread no further among the people, let us warn them to speak no more to any one in this name" (Acts 4:17).

When they tell this to Peter and John, the apostles reply, "Whether it is right in the sight of God to listen to you rather than to God, you must judge; for we cannot but speak of what we have seen and heard" (Acts 4:19-20). •

They are arrested and released on the same day, and once they are free, they go to the brethren and share what has happened and what has been said. They consider the suffering they have endured as a repetition of the cross of Jesus. Then they pray:

> "Lord, look upon their threats, and grant to your servants to speak your word with all boldness, while you stretch out your hand to heal, and signs and wonders are performed through the name of your holy servant Jesus." And when they had prayed, the place in which they were gathered together was shaken; and they were all filled with the Holy Spirit and spoke the word of God with boldness" (Acts 4:29-31).

For Christians, the cross is not an obstacle but the path of redemption—a reenactment, a new instance in our lives of the mystery of the crucified and risen Jesus. ∾

34. The Deceit of Ananias and Sapphira

⁓

The story of Ananias and Sapphira is certainly a powerful episode and one that can be described as mysterious. However, it is important first to examine the context of this event.

Among the first Christians, "the company of those who believed were of one heart and soul, and no one said that any of the things which he possessed was his own, but they had everything in common" (Acts 4:32). This represented a meaningful sense of freedom in the community with regard to one's goods. In the history of the Church, many male and female saints have borne witness to poverty in powerful and significant ways by stripping themselves of their worldly goods. We can think of the desert monks and all the saints who took the vow of poverty. Jesus said that people's lives do not depend on their possessions. In line with Christ's example of poverty, solitary prayer, and fasting, his followers in the early Church believed in and experienced fulfillment quite apart from what they owned, and they learned that "it is more blessed to give than to receive" (Acts 20:35).

Nevertheless, the following event took place in the early Church: "But a man named Ananias with his wife Sapphira sold a piece of property, and with his wife's knowledge he kept back some of the proceeds, and brought only a part and laid it at the apostles' feet" (Acts 5:1-2). This couple was not being honest; they were giving but in the context of fraud. They were not obliged to give; they chose to give, but did so insincerely. Acts tells us that Peter said to them,

"Ananias, why has Satan filled your heart to lie to the Holy Spirit and to keep back part of the proceeds of the land? While it remained unsold, did it not remain your own? And after it was sold, was it not at your disposal? How is it that you have contrived this deed in your heart? You have not lied to men but to God." (Acts 5:3-4)

What a surprising connection Peter makes! Lying to men means lying to God! Every action against others is an offense against God, just as every act of love toward others is an act of love toward God. Jesus said, "As you did it to one of the least of these my brethren, you did it to me" (Matthew 25:40).

It happened that while Ananias and Sapphira were holding something back and being deceptive, God manifested himself through an extraordinary sign. Peter said they had not lied to men but to God. "When Ananias heard these words, he fell down and died. And great fear came upon all who heard of it" (Acts 5:5).

This immediate chastisement is instructive for us. From its beginning, the Church, following Jesus' teaching, was characterized by its culture of giving and its approach to money as an instrument and not an end in itself. This disturbing event signifies that when money becomes an idol, it leads to death and hurts many people. Sapphira, in fact, came to the same end as Ananias did (Acts 5:7-10).

To lie is to mislead. To deceive one's neighbor and, in this case, the Church community represented by Peter, is to break communion. To act outside the community—or worse, against it—does not generate life but initiates a principle of death.

This event also reveals something mysterious about the Church. The message from the following prayer in the psalms now also applies to the Church: "Behold, you desire truth in the inward being" (Psalm 51:6). Looking at Judas' tragic end as well, we can see that when money is an idol, it is indeed a principle of disintegration and death. ∾

35. THE ARREST AND DELIVERANCE
OF THE APOSTLES

The apostles are performing signs and wonders: "The people also gathered from the towns around Jerusalem, bringing the sick and those afflicted with unclean spirits, and they were all healed" (Acts 5:16). The Lord is manifesting his saving, miracle-working presence through Peter.

The inability to see the saving work of God in rescuing the poor from their sicknesses and suffering leads the high priest and his company to have the apostles arrested and thrown into a public prison. "But at night an angel of the Lord opened the prison doors and brought them out and said, 'Go and stand in the temple and speak to the people all the words of this Life'" (Acts 5:19-20).

This rescue by the Most High clarifies the mission of the apostles: they are commanded to preach. The first task of the Church is to proclaim the word of God that is "Spirit and life" (John 6:63). The Gospels are not books of speculative philosophy; instead, they contain "the words of eternal life" (6:68).

The authentic proclamation of the word generates life, the life of God in us. The apostles' arena is the Temple and the streets. When the high priest who thinks the apostles are in prison sends for them, they cannot be found. "And some one came and told them, 'The men whom you put in prison are standing in the temple and teaching the people'" (Acts 5:25).

The captain and his guards go out to bring them back peacefully rather than by force because they fear being stoned by the people. They bring the apostles back to the Sanhedrin, where they are reprimanded with a very significant reproof, but it is a reproof that points to their own psychological fears: "We strictly charged you not to teach in this name, yet here you have filled Jerusalem with your teaching and you intend to bring this man's blood upon us" (Acts 5:28).

Peter stands up and responds together with the other apostles, "We must obey God rather than men" (Acts 5:29). His statement flows from the power of faith. It has made martyrs; it has cast down rulers of this world. Peter's statement reveals the power of faith, which is the power of God.

And then, like a man enthralled by the *kerygma* who does not make intellectual speeches but repeats a refrain, Peter proclaims Jesus yet again: "The God of our fathers raised Jesus whom you killed by hanging him on a tree. God exalted him at his right hand as Leader and Savior, to give repentance to Israel and forgiveness of sins. And we are witnesses to these things, and so is the Holy Spirit whom God has given to those who obey him" (Acts 5:30-32).

Note that in Peter's words there is an attempt at interfaith dialogue when he refers to "the God of *our* fathers." They have a connection: the one and only God and Jesus, a real historical being. And yet there is no real listening or acceptance on the part of the Jewish leaders. Listening to the other diminishes hostility, but when there is no dialogue, aggression and violence emerge. In fact, the passage ends this way: "When they heard this they were enraged and wanted to kill them" (Acts 5:33).

Wanting to kill others for ideological reasons is the most illogical motive that exists in human relationships. Respecting differences is basic civility. It never works to dictate to others; it often works to offer proposals to them. Truth is not absolute in anyone except God. For that reason, whoever kills another human being because of "truth" is always in the wrong. ∾

36. HEALING AND RAISING FROM THE DEAD

∾

The last chapter of Mark's Gospel concludes with Jesus' words as he sends his apostles out into the world:

"Go into all the world and preach the gospel to the whole creation. He who believes and is baptized will be saved; but he who does not believe will be condemned. And these signs will accompany those who believe: in my name they will cast out demons; they will speak in new tongues; they will pick up serpents, and if they drink any deadly thing, it will not hurt them; they will lay their hands on the sick, and they will recover." (Mark 16:15-18)

After the descent of the Holy Spirit, Peter was an evangelist in every way. The signs that were to accompany genuine believers, according to Jesus' word, were manifested in him. At times there are preachers who do not have much faith, but Peter's proclamation of the word came from his great faith and passion for Jesus.

Acts records two episodes concerning Peter that involve the signs Jesus said would accompany believers: a healing and a raising from the dead. Let us look at the healing episode first.

"Now as Peter went here and there among them all, he came down also to the saints that lived at Lydda" (Acts 9:32). It is touching that he visited "them all." This pastoral dimension remains very valid today. The shepherd should go in search of his sheep, especially if they have gone astray. And the *via cordis*, "the way of the heart," surpasses every other method of evangelization.

In Lydda, Peter "found a man named Aeneas, who had been bedridden for eight years and was paralyzed" (Acts 9:33). Paralysis, as we know, immobilizes a person. Peter, in Jesus' name, heals him. The text records it this way: "And Peter said to him, 'Aeneas, Jesus Christ heals you; rise and make your bed.' And immediately he rose. And all the residents of Lydda and Sharon saw him, and they turned to the Lord" (9:34-35).

When someone—in this case, an apostle like Peter—heals a sick person in Jesus' name, it demonstrates the saving power of the Lord who is the power of salvation for the whole human being. People's hearts are moved, and they convert.

Another interesting and moving episode in Acts occurs when Peter raises a woman in Joppa from the dead. In that city, the sacred text says, there was a Christian disciple called Tabitha, which means "gazelle," who was "full of good works and acts of charity" (Acts 9:36). She became ill and died, so the people washed her body and laid it in the upper room.

The text notes, "Since Lydda was near Joppa, the disciples, hearing that Peter was there, sent two men to him entreating him, 'Please come to us without delay'" (Acts 9:38). As soon as Peter arrives in Joppa, he is led to Tabitha's house. At emotional times, memories can surface, so her friends show Peter the coats and garments that Tabitha had made. After that, "Peter put them all outside and knelt down and prayed; then turning to the body he said, 'Tabitha, rise.' And she opened her eyes, and when she saw Peter she sat up" (9:40).

Peter is able to perform signs because of his profound rapport with the Lord. He prays first, and then he says, "Rise." He performs this miracle in the power of the Lord Jesus in an atmosphere of prayer and silence. "Then calling the saints and widows he presented her alive. And it became known throughout all Joppa, and many believed in the Lord" (Acts 9:41-42).

Peter performs this powerful sign against death in the power of the risen One. The signs of God do not come from emotion; they come through and by faith. Faith points toward life. The Lord is stronger than death because he is the Lord of life. Above all, this episode shows us that all the actions of his apostles affirmed life.

"I am the resurrection and the life," Jesus said. "He who believes in me, though he die, yet shall he live" (John 11:25). Jesus' words also apply to the death we have inside of us: "Whoever lives and believes in me shall never die" (11:26). ∽

37. PETER, CORNELIUS, AND THE HOLY SPIRIT

୨

Chapter 10 and 11 of the Acts of the Apostles narrate the event of inclusive baptism, if I can say it that way. Three protagonists in this episode changed history: the Holy Spirit of God; Cornelius, a centurion of the Italian Cohort; and Peter, the leader of the apostles and the guardian of faith in Jesus.

Cornelius is described as "a devout man who feared God with all his household, gave alms liberally to the people, and prayed constantly to God" (Acts 10:2). One day around 3:00 p.m., he has a vision of an angel who tells him to send for a man named Simon, also called Peter, who is lodging with a tanner by the seaside.

Peter, meanwhile, has gone up to the housetop around noon to pray. He becomes hungry, and while his food is being prepared, he falls into a trance. He sees the heavens open and something like a great sheet coming down. "In it were all kinds of animals and reptiles and birds of the air. And there came a voice to him, 'Rise, Peter; kill and eat.' But Peter said, 'No, Lord; for I have never eaten anything that is common or unclean'" (Acts 10:12-14).

On the housetop, Peter hears the voice a second time, and this time it says, "What God has cleansed, you must not call common" (Acts 10:15). This happens a third time, and then finally, "the thing was taken up at once to heaven" (10:16). Peter is actually being exhorted to no longer fear sharing a meal with the uncircumcised. He will say to the people in Cornelius's house the next day, "You yourselves know how unlawful it is for a

Jew to associate with or to visit any one of another nation; but God has shown me that I should not call any man common or unclean" (10:28).

The men sent to find Peter tell him about Cornelius and his angelic vision. When Peter arrives in Caesarea with them the next day, "Cornelius met him and fell down at his feet and worshiped him. But Peter lifted him up, saying, 'Stand up; I too am a man'" (Acts 10:25-26).

When Peter sees the people in Cornelius's household gathered together, he begins to deliver a solemn sermon that is appropriately pastoral. Fulfilling his role as guide of the Church, he speaks out clearly:

> "Truly, I perceive that God show no partiality, but in every nation any one who fears him and does what is right is acceptable to him. You know the word which he sent to the sons of Israel, preaching good news of peace by Jesus Christ (he is Lord of all), the word which was proclaimed throughout all Judea, beginning from Galilee after the baptism which John preached: how God anointed Jesus of Nazareth with the Holy Spirit and with power; how he went about doing good and healing all that were oppressed by the devil, for God was with him. And we are witnesses to all that he did both in the country of the Jews and in Jerusalem. They put him to death by hanging him on a tree; but God raised him on the third day and made him manifest; not to all the people but to us who were chosen by God as witnesses, who ate and drank with him after he rose from the dead. And he commanded us to preach to the people,

and to testify that he is the one ordained by God to be judge of the living and the dead. To him all the prophets bear witness that every one who believes in him receives forgiveness of sins through his name." (Acts 10:34-43)

Peter's speech is a solid outline of the content of the Church's fundamental preaching. Peter, the fisherman who is now a teacher through his divine calling, is the one on the front lines of the most burning issues at the Church's beginning. His magisterial status, inspired by the Spirit, is confirmed here:

While Peter was still saying this, the Holy Spirit fell on all who heard the word. And the believers from among the circumcised who came with Peter were amazed, because the gift of the Holy Spirit had been poured out even on the Gentiles. For they heard them speaking in tongues and extolling God. Then Peter declared, "Can any one forbid water for baptizing these people who have received the Holy Spirit just as we have?" And he commanded them to be baptized in the name of Jesus Christ. (Acts 10:44-48).

The head of the apostolic college handled this crucial time in the early Church though divine inspiration. The humble fisherman from Galilee, enlightened by the Spirit, emerges here as a guide for the Church and a bright signpost for history. ∾

38. Peter's Explanations in Jerusalem

༄

In the text from Acts for our reflection (11:1-18), it is already clear that in the early Church, no decisions for the community were made privately. The Church was, in fact, communal. There could be personal choices illuminated by prayer, but they needed to be in harmony with the direction of the community.

The very significant turning point of opening the Church to the Gentiles had given rise to many reactions. For that reason, some of the people in Jerusalem questioned Peter, saying, "Why did you go to uncircumcised men and eat with them?" (Acts 11:3).

Peter recounts his experiences in detail. He talks about the vision and the voice that told him not to call common what God had made clean. He emphasizes that it was all the work of the Holy Spirit. When the three men from Caesarea had come to find him, "the Spirit told me to go with them, making no distinction" (Acts 11:12).

Peter had been accompanied by six of his brethren from Joppa, and Cornelius had shared his vision with them as well. The Lord acts in so many ways to bring about unity. Peter says, "As I began to speak, the Holy Spirit fell on them just as on us at the beginning. And I remembered the word of the Lord, how he said, 'John baptized with water, but you shall be baptized with the Holy Spirit.' If then God gave the same gift to them as he gave to us when we believed in the Lord Jesus Christ, who was I that I could withstand God?" (Acts 11:15-17). After hearing Peter, the Jerusalem brethren were silenced, and "they glorified God, saying, 'Then to the Gentiles also God has granted repentance unto life'" (11:18).

Four points emerge from this episode and Peter's narrative. First, there is the work of the Holy Spirit in guiding the Church. The Spirit is a living presence, seemingly hidden but clearly active and bringing inspiration.

Second, the Spirit led Peter to change his thinking about an issue that he was not considering and that he even opposed. This is instructive to help contextualize and illuminate our own actions in the Church.

Next, the community is seen as living and active. Peter did not impose his ideas but engaged in dialogue and communicated. The exercise of authority in the Church does not occur in a vacuum; the Church listens, evaluates, and decides. When it speaks, it does not do so high-handedly; it communicates by teaching God's ways. Above all, it acts in conjunction with the Spirit who guides its decisions.

Finally, a revelatory word from God is an inescapable reference point: "I *remembered the word of the Lord*," Peter says (Acts 11:16, emphasis added). The word of God is a guarantee and a comfort. It quiets a range of different views and unifies people's thinking to be in line with God's thinking.

The Lord is again speaking to the ones whom we call "far off," the "pagans" of our time. God is over all and in all. A believing heart knows that God is great and marvelous, and he is always surprising us. These are perennial truths taught by the Church. We need, of course, to discuss issues, but we need, above all, to listen to the Spirit together and, in him, to listen to those whom we might consider "on the margins." ∽

39. PETER IN CHAINS

In 2 Corinthians 4:7-10, Paul affirms, "We have this treasure in earthen vessels, to show that the transcendent power belongs to God and not to us. We are afflicted in every way, but not crushed; perplexed, but not driven to despair; persecuted, but not forsaken; struck down, but not destroyed; always carrying in the body the death of Jesus, so that the life of Jesus may also be manifested in our bodies."

Peter, along with the other apostles, experienced persecution—chains for the kingdom of God. Acts of the Apostles records these times of violence and injustice against those who were proclaiming the gospel: "Herod the king laid violent hands upon some who belonged to the Church. He killed James the brother of John with the sword" (12:1-2). As so often happens to leaders who are affected by ill-formed public opinion, "When he saw that it pleased the Jews, he proceeded to arrest Peter also" (12:3).

It is disheartening when a person who is appointed to oversee the common good and bring justice for all allows himself to be guided by the crowd, which is always moved by whims and various political or ideological influences. Herod put Peter in prison "and delivered him to four squads of soldiers to guard him, intending after the Passover to bring him out to the people" (Acts 12:4).

Everything was planned. However, the power of God is greater and stronger than the injustices of oppressors. In this case, while the ruling powers are doing their plotting, the Church is in constant prayer for Peter. While preparations are being made to bring

Peter before the people, the Lord demonstrates that the prison system cannot hinder his own plans.

Peter is being watched by soldiers and is bound with two chains; sentries are guarding the door of the prison. As he is sleeping, "An angel of the Lord appeared, and a light shone in the cell" (Acts 12:7). Cells are normally dingy and gloomy, but the light of God appears in this dark prison. The angel touches Peter's side to wake him and says, "Get up quickly" (12:7).

Angels are messengers from God. They are creatures that are above human beings, and God sends messages through them. We can remember the angel of the Annunciation and the angels at Jesus' resurrection. It is comforting that God speaks and acts through his angels.

The text goes on to tell of Peter's liberation by the mighty hand of God and reports more of the angel's words: "'Dress yourself and put on your sandals.' And he did so. And he said to him, 'Wrap your cloak around you and follow me.' And he went out and followed him; he did not know that what was done by the angel was real, but thought he was seeing a vision" (Acts 12:8-9).

It might be intriguing to examine the difference between a vision and reality, but it is uplifting to see a gloomy reality from the perspective of the beauty of God's continual movement. God is not merely a dream. "My Father is working still," Jesus said, "and I am working" (John 5:17). Reality can become boring, burdensome, and, at times, mundane for us if we do not see the Love that cares for us, that accompanies us, that opens the doors of so many of our prisons.

Peter and the angel walk past the first and second guards and arrive at the iron gate leading out to the city. "It opened to them of its own accord, and they went out and passed on through one street; and immediately the angel left him" (Acts 12:10).

Peter realizes that he is not dreaming and says, "Now I am sure that the Lord has sent his angel and rescued me from the hand of Herod and from all that the Jewish people were expecting" (Acts 12:11). The certainty that God is at work brings inner liberation from every kind of prison and causes us to celebrate a life of love in our freedom as children of God.

Peter has left his family for Jesus, and now he is surrounded by a community of believers. He knocks at the door of the house of Mary, the mother of John (also called Mark), where many people are gathered in prayer. Where there is prayer, there are people looking to heaven, and for that reason they see the earth more clearly.

As Peter knocks, a young woman named Rhoda comes to the gate. Hearing Peter's voice, she is so bewildered in her joy that she fails to open the gate. It is comforting to see that Scriptures describe human emotions and reactions. It seems to me that its historicity is confirmed through these kinds of details.

Peter enters the house and "motioning to them with his hand to be silent, he described to them how the Lord had brought him out of the prison. And he said, 'Tell this to James and to the brethren'" (Acts 12:17).

Herod, unable to understand the workings of God, questions the sentries and has them put to death (cf. Acts 12:19). The tyrannical man finds it hard to understand certain events and assumes he can resolve all things with brute force. The plans of God are like a tapestry whose design is on the reverse side, and his plans destroy pride and the misuse of power. ∽

40. PETER'S INTERVENTION
IN A CONTROVERSY

ာ

One of the tasks of the early Church was to discern the link between the Christian faith and circumcision, which was the sign of faith in the God of Israel. According to Acts, "Some men came down from Judea and were teaching the brethren, 'Unless you are circumcised according to the custom of Moses, you cannot be saved'" (15:1).

Paul and Barnabas strongly oppose this position. In an example of ecclesial unity and faith, the community decides that Paul, Barnabas, and others will go to Jerusalem to present the issue to the apostles and elders. They go through Phoenicia and Samaria, "reporting the conversion of the Gentiles, and they gave great joy to all the brethren" (Act 15:3).

They are welcomed in Jerusalem, where they report on the apostolic work they had done. However, some people there from the sect of the Pharisees who had become Christians are also insisting on the need for circumcision and on the keeping of the Mosaic law.

The apostles and elders gather to discuss the matter. After a long and difficult discussion, Peter, the head of the Church, rises up and says,

"Brethren, you know that in the early days God made choice among you, that by my mouth the Gentiles should hear the word of the gospel and believe. And God who knows the heart bore witness to them, giving them the Holy Spirit just as he did to us; and he made no distinction between us and them, but cleansed their hearts by faith. Now therefore why do you make trial of God by putting a yoke upon the neck of the disciples which neither our fathers nor we have been able to bear? But we believe that we shall be saved through the grace of the Lord Jesus, just as they will." (Acts 15:7-11)

Peter's speech is fluent and goes to the heart of the matter. He explains that the word of God has granted the gift of the Holy Spirit to pagans as well. God, who knows people's hearts, does not want discrimination against any group.

God purifies everyone's heart through faith. Faith is like an antenna that people have to receive the God who is the Lord of all, and receiving him is the beginning of salvation. God does not distinguish between people based on earthly criteria, such as biological family, race, or group membership, but on the level and measure of their faith.

Peter, seeing the stubbornness of some of the people there, forcefully says, "Why do you make trial of God?" (Acts 15:10) and reminds them that both Jews and Gentiles will be saved through grace. What does "making trial of God" mean? It means trying to bring God over to our point of view, trying to use him. I believe that it is a sin, a widespread sin that often goes unnoticed. But God transcends us; he will not be used. Above all, he is not drawn to our ideas—or worse, to our preferences and plans. God is to be welcomed; he does not let himself be used as an instrument.

Once more in apostolic teaching, the inclusive character of salvation was being asserted. God gives himself to all. He is, as Paul says, the "Father of us all, who is above all and through all and in all" (Ephesians 4:6). We presumptuously project our limitations onto him when our categorizations try to put him in a box.

Peter's ministry was instead compassionate, enlightened by the visions he had. He affirmed the inclusive nature of the salvation that descends from the one Father, the one Lord, the one Spirit of love and unity. ∽

41. A Summary of the First Letter of Peter

～

Two of the seven catholic epistles in the New Testament carry Peter's name. The first is addressed to Christians in the diaspora. It names the recipients as being among the faithful in Asia Minor and those dispersed in Pontus, Galatia, Cappadocia, Asia, and Bithynia (1 Peter 1:1).

Peter is writing from Rome, which he calls Babylon (1 Peter 5:13). This name is clearly linked to Rome when it appears in Revelation 14:8, 16:19, and 17:5. He is assisted by Silvanus, whom he calls a "faithful brother" (1 Peter 5:12). Silvanus is the one who will deliver the letter; some scholars believe that he was not only a messenger but also this letter's writer under the direction of the apostle. In any case, the purpose of both letters is clear: they are meant to encourage the faith of Christians who are undergoing trials.

The letters contain very precise and clear articulations that we could call "the first Christian theology"—for example, Peter's reflection on the redemptive value of the Lord's death, the link between faith and baptism, and so forth. My purpose in commenting on his letters is pastoral; it is not to offer a doctrinal or exegetical teaching, but to present Peter, the head of the Church, as a "teacher of faith."

Peter's first letter is clearly contextualized for the time it was written, but it also applies for all times, including ours. Since my book aims at Christian meditation, I have selected the points that allow me to offer practical reflections for the life of a Christian and the life of the Church today.

1. *A Lively Hope* (1 Peter 1:3-5)

We can enter into the mystery of God only as we open our hearts to welcome him. God is not reached as we try to ascend to him through a Promethean struggle; he is found when we are on our knees, knowing and experiencing him as the giver of every gift (James 1:17). That is why biblical letters very often begin with blessing God. To bless God is to receive him and to express gratitude for his work in our lives.

Peter blesses God because he has given us new life through the resurrection of Jesus. That new life is our hope; it is a dynamic life that is always new because Jesus is alive forever and intercedes for us. The face of God who awaits us is our hope; it is reserved for us in heaven.

The power of God guards us on earth through faith. Faith is the surrender of our lives to the power of God at work in us.

2. *Joy* (1 Peter 1:6-9)

Peter tells us to be overflowing with joy. Having joy, then, is not just a possibility but something we are called to have. Joy is not so much an inner state as it is a presence, the presence of the Lord. He is present in the midst of our trials. In fact, it is in our crosses that we experience his resurrection. Peter says that faith is more precious than gold. It is the light of life; it is the root of hope. Faith says, "God is with me"; hope says, "God will always come."

Peter sees the resurrection of the Lord as giving us the hope of the inheritance that is kept in heaven for us. "If we are children of God, then we are heirs of God" (cf. Romans 8:17).

3. *The Prophets and the Spirit* (1 Peter 1:10-12)

Peter's letter is like a magnet that picks up other things as it moves around. With each pronouncement, his letter breaks out into new directions. It not only makes concise, fundamental statements, but it also elaborates them in a way that develops them and thus demonstrates the inexhaustibility of truth.

The prophets, he says, tried to inquire about the sufferings and the glory of Christ, and they received revelation, not only for themselves, but also for us and for all times.

4. *The New Life* (1 Peter 1:13-21)

There is a need for depth today, but there is no depth without an inner life. People steeped in the contemplation of God can fix their gaze on the hope of the grace that will be given to us when Christ will be revealed.

This letter is filled with hope—what Peter calls a "living hope" (1 Peter 1:3). Christian hope is Christ himself; it is anything but a mere dream. We see the continual coming of God as we await the fullness of his final coming. Hope is rooted in faith that the Lord is with us, even—and most importantly—in our trials. Christ is the present-but-hidden One.

Peter's letter calls us to holiness as he recalls the words of Leviticus 19:2: "You shall be holy, for I am holy" (1:16). Human beings were created in the image and likeness of God. Because of sin, we need to be reconciled to God through Christ so that we again become reflections of the Lord. If people do not rediscover themselves in Christ, they are not fulfilled. They have no peace and they have no life.

Peter tells us, "Conduct yourselves with fear throughout the time of your exile" (1 Peter 1:17). Fear here does not mean an anxious state of fright. It refers to the quiet and often difficult task of guarding our love. It means keeping watch and being alert in caring for our souls.

Here is another invitation to contemplate the price of our redemption. We were not bought with gold or silver, which is the world's way of buying and selling, but with the precious blood of Christ who is like a lamb without spot or blemish. The blood of Christ is what washes and cleanses all of us.

The mention of Christ as the Lamb is a reference to a symbol that occurs in the Old and New Testaments. The Lamb is the ultimate Word: "And I saw no temple in the city, for its temple is the Lord God the Almighty and the Lamb. And the city has no need of sun or moon to shine upon it, for the glory of God is its light, and its lamp is the Lamb" (Revelation 21:22-23). History is reborn through the cross. It is not charted by the invasion of wolves but by the silent offering of the sacrificed Lamb.

5. *Regeneration through the Living and Abiding Word of God*
(1 Peter 1:22-25)
We frequently speak about the paths for the sanctification of our souls. Peter shows us two very interesting ways to achieve holiness. The first is "obedience to the truth," and the second is "a sincere love of the brethren" (1 Peter 1:22).

Christian truth does not develop into its fullness as we reflect on it; it is an attribute of God that is revealed to us. The God of Jesus is "living and true" (1 Thessalonians 1:9). Jesus told us, "I am the way, and the truth, and the life" (John 14:6). Obeying the truth is saying yes to God. We can recall here the example of Mary, the Lord's mother, who said, "Behold, I am the handmaid of the Lord; let it be to me according to your word" (Luke 1:38).

The other path, which is like the fulfillment of truth, is love. Peter speaks about earnest, sincere love. That earnestness comes from a deep relationship with the Lord. Teaching about love, John tells us, "He who does not love his brother whom he has seen, cannot love God whom he has not seen" (1 John 4:20).

6. *The Milk of the Spirit and the New Priesthood* (1 Peter 2:1-10) This passage is very dense but instructive. It begins along the line of Jesus' saying that "unless you turn and become like children, you will never enter the kingdom of heaven" (Matthew 18:3). Jesus does not ask us to be children but to become *like* children. To succeed in being carried by God and entrusting ourselves to him is the fruit of great asceticism and purification of heart.

A child leaps into its parents' arms. Peter asks us to make that leap while embracing Christ, whom he calls a "living stone" (1 Peter 2:4). I commented earlier in the introduction that this is a wonderful image. The phrase could be paraphrased this way: Jesus is someone to lean on who is sweet and refreshing. Unfortunately, people look for other kinds of support and reject him.

The text next says, "Like living stones be yourselves built into a spiritual house, to be a holy priesthood" (1 Peter 2:5). This priesthood is not ministerial but spiritual. It belongs to all believers so that they can build up a life of love and communion, but primarily so that they can offer themselves through Jesus.

7. *Christian Conduct toward Nonbelievers* (1 Peter 2:11-12)

Peter does not have a homogeneous, predetermined theme in either letter. Each includes very deep sections on a variety of issues that are not always linked to the basic discussion at hand and seem to erupt in spontaneous contemplation.

In verse 11, Peter says that believers on earth are like "aliens and exiles." That is an excellent description. We are not yet in our permanent homeland but are en route to our homeland. We are also in the midst of trials as we experience the desires of the flesh warring with our souls.

What is the flesh? It is linked not only to our bodies but also to the "I" that puts itself first, shunning the guidance of the Spirit who integrates, strengthens, and lifts up human beings.

8. *The Believer and Authority* (1 Peter 2:13-17)

This compact summary from Peter has a wealth of teaching about a very current issue: the relationship of Christians to the authority of the state and their conduct and activity in secular society.

First, Peter links this relationship to the Lord of love. Because of this love, Christians are to be respectful of all legitimate human institutions. Christians also contribute to history, applying the leaven of the divine word to complex situations in the world.

Peter then exhorts Christians once more to conduct themselves as free men. "Freedom" is perhaps the most abused word and the most misunderstood concept today. Freedom does not mean breaking away from every accepted standard and authority; that only leads to an overindulgence of our egos and our whims.

True freedom must be won. Freedom does not work in opposition to truth but is the actualization of truth. True freedom is creative in how it leads us to serve others in truth and love.

9. *Blessings in Suffering for God* (1 Peter 2:18-25)

Peter speaks to servants, exhorting them to have respect for their masters, and not just for the ones who are kind, gentle, and understanding, but also for the overbearing ones.

At this point, he deals with unjust suffering. He does so by pointing to Jesus, the one who did not commit sin but nevertheless suffered for us. Peter contemplates Christ as he stood silently before the injustices against him, having abandoned himself to God while representing sinful human beings. The text says he "bore our sins" (1 Peter 2:24).

What a lesson on such a crucial point in our Christian experience! Unjust suffering often makes us lose our temper. Angry thoughts enter in, and our former charitable attitude disappears.

The altruistic attitude of Jesus is the model: although innocent, he carried the sins of the world through love, and as the Lamb of God, he bore these sins in himself. Unfortunately, this model of innocent suffering is not often followed.

In history people of two types emerge: those who make others suffer and those who suffer for the wrongdoing of others and remain silent. Jesus offered himself for them and for us all. For the Christian, this paradoxical innovation is beyond all human logic and reason.

Jesus, who is unconditional love par excellence, suffered and offered himself for the unrighteous although he was righteous. Similarly, Christians, if they are mature, do not curse unjust suffering but offer it for the redemption of others. Christian holiness leads people to take on the burdens of others. In contrast, people living apart from Christ complain about pain and curse everything and everyone.

Innocent suffering out of love is a source of joy; arguing against suffering, resisting it, becomes a source of anxiety. The former is constructive; the latter is destructive to oneself and to others.

10. *The Ethics and Spirituality of Marriage* (1 Peter 3:1-7)
Peter offers a general survey of many situations in life. He now makes a comment on the marital relationship. Marriage is an original creation by God. It is a total sharing of life; it is a reflection of communion in the Godhead.

Peter, being aware of the culture of his time, first addresses the woman. This is not—as some have hastily concluded—because the woman causes the downfall of marriage but, on the contrary, because she is an instrument of domestic harmony. Feminine spirituality is already oriented toward the gift of self. It is not what she says that is significant but who she is. Peter remarks that if the wife is quiet, chaste, and respectful, even if she does not use words, she is a constructive presence for the family and for domestic harmony. There is a chastity of soul as well as a chastity of the body.

Peter then turns to husbands to tell them how to care for their wives and support them with deep, respectful love. Given the discord in so many families today, Peter's call is for couples to return to respecting the essential and existential aspects of man and woman and their different psychologies. This can lead, through faith, to constructive and peaceful behaviors.

11. *An Expression of Community Love* (1 Peter 3:8-12)
This passage invites us to a unity that can be concretely attained: it calls for our participation in the joys and sorrows of others. True charity means treating others as ourselves and knowing how to share our lives. People should not feel that they are on their own when they are among Christians. Compassion means having a heart for the needs of others. Peter points to humility here as the fertile ground for charity.

12. *The Beatitude of Persecution* (1 Peter 3:13-17)
The early Church experienced persecution. Peter takes up one of Jesus' beatitudes—"Blessed are those who are persecuted for righteousness' sake, for theirs is the kingdom of heaven" (Matthew 5:10)—and phrases it this way: "If you do suffer for righteousness' sake, you will be blessed. Have no fear" (1 Peter 3:14). Peter points to a very safe refuge. If we accept the suffering of persecution, we will always truly be at peace and have joy in our trials: "[Do not] be troubled, but in your hearts reverence Christ as Lord" (3:14-15).

Peter invites us to be ready in responding to whoever asks us about the reason for the hope that is in us. Even in times of temptation and difficult circumstances, we should conduct ourselves with kindness, gentleness, and respect for others.

13. *The Proclamation of the Central Event of Our Faith* (1 Peter 3:18-22)
This section contains all the elements of an ancient profession of faith: the death of Christ, his descent into hell, his resurrection, his sitting at the right hand of the Father, and his judgment of the

living and the dead. It is an edifying summary, and one of its rich assertions is that Christ was "put to death in the flesh but made alive in the spirit" (1 Peter 3:18).

Peter takes a brief look at the Old Testament and that phase in salvation history when God was dealing with many infidelities against himself. There is, however, the proclamation of the victory of the love of God.

Noah's ark is seen as a symbol of salvation. Peter sees in the ark a figure of baptism that now saves us from the flood of the world. Baptism, he says, is not like the water that removes the body's filth; it is an appeal addressed to God for a clean conscience. Baptism is a gift of salvation that flows from the resurrection of the Lord Jesus.

14. *Breaking with Sin* (1 Peter 4:1-6)

Christ is the man of sorrows. His disciples must carry their cross as he did: "If any man would come after me, let him deny himself and take up his cross and follow me" (Mark 8:34).

We are asked not merely to tolerate the cross, or worse, to curse it, but to have in ourselves the same attitude that was in Christ Jesus. What was his attitude? Looking at the cross, Jesus called it *his* cross. It was not forced on him, and he did not react against it. Instead, he awaited it. He looked at it as the culmination of his love for us and of his faithfulness to God's plan. Thus, all Christians should understand how to accept their suffering and offer that pain for their own redemption and for that of all human beings.

Taking up the cross means changing our direction. It means not following our passions and, instead, renouncing worldly pleasures that numb and deaden us.

15. *Awaiting the Parousia* (1 Peter 4:7-11)

Peter's letter covers a variety of issues in a way that is simultaneously doctrinal and practical. In this passage, starting off with the idea that "the end of all things is at hand," he indicates the paths that a Christian should walk while awaiting the end (1 Peter 4:7).

His vision does not focus on apocalyptic imminence but on the precariousness of life on earth and of visible things. We are now *viatores*, pilgrims; we see as though in a mirror. Soon we will see God as he is.

As I said, the text here does not stress the imminence of the Parousia. However, given that "a thousand years in your sight / are but as yesterday when it is past" (Psalm 90:4), the Parousia, which sheds light on everything in the present, also simultaneously points to the last things. For that reason, Peter exhorts people to keep a balance, given that the visible is transitory, and he invites us to devote ourselves to prayer.

Devotion to prayer is a consecration that leads to a genuine life of prayer. Everything we do should involve prayer. Prayer does not mean retreating from life; prayer illuminates life, integrates it, and lifts it up to God. Prayer is implicit when it is at the heart of every action that leads to our "being and living" in the Lord.

Prayer brings us extraordinary peace, joy in everything, and the fulfillment of all things. People who make their lives a prayer enjoy every aspect of existence: joy and sorrow, work and rest, and so forth. It fulfills the command to "abide in me" (John 15:4) that Jesus gave us.

United to God through prayer, we can maintain continual charity among ourselves. Continual charity means that charity

WALKING ON WATER WITH ST. PETER

is not merely a repeated gesture but, rather, an inner disposition toward all of life.

16. *The Beatitude of Suffering in Christ* (1 Peter 4:12-19)
Peter is writing at a time when the early Church is undergoing severe trials of persecution. The last beatitude recorded in Matthew's Gospel says, "Blessed are those who are persecuted for righteousness' sake, for theirs is the kingdom of heaven" (5:10). The persecution of Christians, which is provoked because their lives are signs of contradiction, is a participation in the sufferings of Christ that redeem the world.

In this passage Peter indicates the twofold source of suffering. The apostle clearly tells us that we also suffer when we do evil. He affirms, "Let none of you suffer as a murderer, or a thief, or a wrongdoer, or a mischief-maker" (1 Peter 4:15). There is a suffering due to sin and a suffering because of truth. God's light distinguishes between the two.

However, if people suffer as Christians, there is obviously no shame in that, and they should glorify God. If we are true Christians, we will be persecuted and we will glory in the name of God. That kind of suffering is the seed of life and of resurrection.

17. *Exhortations to the Elders and to the Faithful* (1 Peter 5:1-10)
This first exhortation, to the elders (1 Peter 5:1-4), is brief but very rich. It is a clear summary that sets forth the inner life, the asceticism, and the pastoral conduct of elders that are necessary for all times and all places. Peter is not speaking to the elders from a position of superiority because he calls himself "a fellow elder and a witness of the suffering of Christ as well as a partaker in

the glory that is to be revealed" (5:1). He then exhorts them to "tend the flock of God that is your charge" (5:2).

The flock belongs to God. It is not ours; it has been entrusted to us. This initial point is very important and inescapable for all those who are called to pastoral ministry. We are, after all, only "unworthy servants" (Luke 17:10).

The flock is his. He alone is the Shepherd. We are not acting in our name but *in nomine Christi*, "in Christ's name." No one should put himself or herself forward or try to avoid what a minister actually is: a servant of the flock, in the name of the Lord.

The second exhortation (1 Peter 5:5) is to those who are "younger," who are known as "neophytes," that is, all those who are not the elders who guide the Church. Their submission is spiritual. They are to be docile in receiving teaching with hearts open to the maturing of their faith.

Peter says that the foundational virtue for the building up of Christian life and Christian community is humility (1 Peter 5:6). Humility is not a disparaging view of oneself but a truthful view that helps every person understand how best to be of service in God's work. The genuine believer is responsive to God, his truth, and his will. We need to resist the evil one, firm in our faith as we experience the suffering common to all believers in the mystery of the world's redemption. ❧

42. A SUMMARY OF THE SECOND LETTER OF PETER

∽

1. *The Greeting* (2 Peter 1:1-2)
Peter calls himself "a servant and apostle of Jesus Christ" (2 Peter 1:1). A servant is someone who depends on his master. Being a servant of Jesus, however, does not signify being a slave. It is a bonded relationship for the sake of the gospel and for the renewal of history: "Behold, I make all things new" (Revelation 21:5).

"Apostle" is a widespread term today, but at the beginning of Christianity it was a title reserved for the Twelve. Because of that, this word will always have a unique meaning.

2. *God's Initiative* (2 Peter 1:3-11)
The power of God is manifested primarily in Jesus. He prays, "Father, the hour has come; glorify your Son that the Son may glorify you, since you have given him power over all flesh, to give eternal life to all whom you have given him" (John 17:1-2).

In Jesus we have been given every good thing that pertains to life and holiness. Paul also makes this point when he says that "the grace of God has appeared for the salvation of all men, training us to renounce irreligion and worldly passions, and to live sober, upright, and godly lives in this world, awaiting our blessed hope, the appearing of the glory of our great God and Savior Jesus Christ" (Titus 2:11-13).

Through the power of Christ, we have been given great and precious blessings so that we may become "partakers of the divine nature" (2 Peter 1:4). The Greek fathers rightly spoke of the "deification" of human beings, a gift flowing from the "humanization of God in Christ." This describes the new life in Christ, the transfer of God's own life to us. John affirms, "But to all who received him, who believed in his name, he gave power to become children of God; who were born, not of blood nor of the will of the flesh nor of the will of man, but of God" (John 1:12-13).

To be Christians, therefore, does not mean adherence to doctrine; it does not mean merely living a moral life. It means "reliving" a filial relationship in all things, thereby becoming sons and daughters in the Son. That is why we should not be conformed to the world's perspective, which is rooted in pride, sensuality, cupidity, vanity, and so forth.

Peter presents his own faith walk and his enthusiasm about the core of Christian life: we are indwelt by God, grafted into Christ, and made temples of the Holy Spirit. He writes about Christian life in an increasingly climactic way. We need to grow, he says, by supplementing "faith with virtue, and virtue with knowledge, and knowledge with self-control, and self-control with steadfastness, and steadfastness with godliness, and godliness with brotherly affection, and brotherly affection with love" (2 Peter 1:5-7). This is the path that helps us avoid having our faith become lifeless and our love become cold. It is an ascetic path that calls for constancy. Paul tells Timothy, "An athlete is not crowned unless he competes according to the rules" (2 Timothy 2:5).

To live this way is to sincerely confirm our call as believers. Entrance into the eternal kingdom will thus be fully available to us; the opening of the "narrow door" (Luke 13:24; cf. Matthew 7:13) will thereby be assured to us.

3. *Peter's Exhortation to Vigilance* (2 Peter 1:12-15)

In this passage Peter reveals the deep transformation of his humanity in Christ as well as his shepherd's heart. He sounds almost like Paul, who writes to the Corinthians, "Though you have countless guides in Christ, you do not have many fathers" (1 Corinthians 4:15). Peter exhorts people to be strong in the truth they have heard. He also wants them to be vigilant about recalling his exhortations, "since I know that the putting off of my body will be soon, as our Lord Jesus Christ showed me" (2 Peter 1:14).

4. *The Epiphany at Tabor* (2 Peter 1:16-21)

This section has great theological and pastoral value. Peter, with great boldness—one of his defining qualities—says that he did not invent clever myths when he made Christ known to them. He recalls and describes for them the light on Tabor and the word of the Father that he personally heard during that astounding vision: "We were eyewitnesses," he says (2 Peter 1:16). Jesus "received honor and glory from God the Father and the voice was borne to him by the Majestic Glory, 'This is my beloved Son, with whom I am well pleased'" (1:17). Peter saw and heard all this because "we were with him on the holy mountain" (1:18).

This was one of Jesus' theophanies. He lived a hidden life; he worked mysteriously and quietly, not caring about people's approval. However, shortly before the horrific event of his passion, he manifested himself in this epiphany of light and glory.

5. *False Teachers* (2 Peter 2:1-3)

The Church also experiences sufferings and trials from within. There is, as we well know, our great conflict with the world in terms of "worldliness," that is, with people who are blind to all but the visible, the rational, and the practical. This calls for a high degree of patience on our part. However, within the community, just as in Peter's time, false prophets and teachers rise up from time to time who introduce "destructive heresies" (2 Peter 2:1). Believers who should be humble and teachable but are not always so can become presumptuous.

If people are not grounded in the truth, false prophets will appoint themselves as interpreters of the word, presuming to interpret it according to their perspective. Such people do not serve Scripture but use it to their advantage. The Church needs humble and docile sons and daughters. People who are not humble readily reveal their conceitedness and their sense of self-importance. Peter notes that "many will follow their licentiousness," and he concludes that "because of them the way of truth will be reviled" (2 Peter 2:2). We need to be vigilant about false teachers who "exploit you with false words" (2:3).

6. *Lessons from the Past* (2 Peter 2:4-10a)

Peter now presents lessons from the Old Testament. He talks about the rebellious angels who were cast into deep pits of darkness in hell. He talks about the flood brought upon the world of the ungodly and the condemnation of Sodom and Gomorrah. All these examples deal with those who lived unrighteous lives.

People say that history is a guide to life. The biblical narratives teach us about faith. Outside of God nothing holds up and everything moves toward destruction. Hell turns everything upside down and inside out. The current ethical breakdown, including the vulgar degradation of the dignity of man and woman, reveals, in an upside-down, reversed way, the very truth of God about men and women.

7. *Future Punishment* (2 Peter 2:10b-22)

Peter's language is very poetic, but his message is very serious: "These are waterless springs and mists driven by a storm; for them the deepest gloom of darkness has been reserved" (2 Peter 1:17). With their hearts full of lust, the arrogant and self-confident carouse in the daytime and are destroyed by their own corruption; they are sons and daughters of malediction and are destined to perish. To live apart from God, inflated by pride, is the downfall of a person's existence.

A strictly horizontal ethic, which is often reduced merely to social problems, shrinks the arena of morality and locks people into the visible. Today we no longer speak about the last things. Obviously, it is not good to cause fear and stress, but ignoring the vertical dimension of ethics and morality leads to superficiality.

We are not destined to have our end on earth; we are called to the eternal One. We need to contemplate him and subsequently make our choice. Life and death are set before us. We have before us either abundance or emptiness. It is obvious that the measure of a person's education and inner enlightenment enters into play. It is also true that the evil one turns our values upside down so that truth is viewed as a lie and wrongdoing is viewed as a legitimate life experience.

Peter, at the Church's beginning, offers us a map for our journey with the compass of faith. He calls us back to the seriousness of life so that we do not drown in deceit or, in traditional language, so that we do not "lose our souls."

8. *Reminders of Prophetic and Apostolic Sayings* (2 Peter 3:1-2)
Peter, in his informative and typically pastoral style, exhorts us to
have a "sincere mind" (2 Peter 3:1), because the mind is powerful
and can be presumptuous. It can think of its role as determina-
tive rather than as humbly accepting truth. We need to keep in
mind the predictions of the prophets and the apostles' teachings.

9. *The Day of the Lord* (2 Peter 3:3-10)
Peter looks at the fulfillment of history in this enlightening text
founded on the sayings of the prophets. There are clear truths here
about "the last days" (2 Peter 3:3). As he teaches on this issue,
he has surprising insights that apply to our spiritual lives as we
wait with vigilance.

The apostle warns us about how to read Scripture. We are not
to use it pragmatically or, worse, opportunistically; we are to contemplate it in its mystery *in lumine fidei*, "in the light of faith." He
corrects the superficiality of those who wait for the Lord's final
coming without considering its unforeseen and mysterious nature.

Jesus said, "You know neither the day nor the hour" (Matthew 25:13). Peter speaks of foolish mockers who ask, "Where
is the promise of his coming?" (2 Peter 3:4). This is certainly a
reference to an eschatological vision that was soon to be fulfilled,
according to a letter being circulated at that time. Peter exhorts
us to have patience and humility before this mystery that belongs
only to God.

Life, then, does not consist in counting down the clock. Life is
received as the seed of eternity in the depths of our hearts. More
than merely registering the passing of time, we need to see God's

action in it. There is a mysterious significance to events, and we need to have our hearts alert to the movements of God.

Vigilance is needed because of the seriousness of the human journey. The Lord does not want anyone to perish, Peter says. However, he also tells us to be aware that "the day of the Lord will come like a thief" (2 Peter 3:10). He says this not to frighten us but to encourage us to be alert and prepared.

10. *The Invitation to New Life and Concluding Doxology* (2 Peter 3:11-18)

"We wait for new heavens and a new earth in which righteousness dwells" (2 Peter 3:13). This is what Peter says we are waiting for from the Lord.

The day of the Lord is eternity—the first and last day, "the day without sunset," as the Liturgy of the Hours says. We are not waiting for a deceptive dream. Eternity will be the fulfillment of history in the presence of God. The text says, "Since you wait for these [things], be zealous to be found by him without spot or blemish, and at peace" (2 Peter 3:14)—we do not want to arrive there with our "baggage." After that, Peter makes the following startling statement: "Count the forbearance of our Lord as salvation" (3:15).

My comment on the above-mentioned verse is that the Lord wants all to be saved. God does not judge according to human standards; his heart is immense. It is true that everyone is in need of mercy, but it is also true that our hope, flowing from our faith, is that "the LORD is . . . slow to anger and abounding in mercy" (Psalm 103:8). God knows the secrets of people's hearts; he became man and took on our limitations. And God considers people's good intentions.

At this point, Peter refers to Paul, who is a messenger of God's mercy. Paul says, in fact, that "he saved us, not because of deeds done by us in righteousness, but in virtue of his own mercy, by the washing of regeneration and renewal in the Holy Spirit" (Titus 3:5). With great nuanced subtlety, Peter notes that because Paul's writing is not simple, "the ignorant and unstable twist [it] to their own destruction" (2 Peter 3:16). ∞

CONCLUSION AND DEDICATION

I see Peter as a living stone for faithful believers but also for anyone who is sincerely and humbly seeking the Lord. Like a rock, Peter is a steady support, someone we can lean on. As we approach him, we can experience God, our rock, "the Rock of your refuge," as Isaiah 17:10 calls him.

I close by repeating the moving prayer from Psalm 16:11:

> You show me the path of life;
>   in your presence there is fullness of joy,
>   in your right hand are pleasures for evermore.

Peter is still alive, now and forever, through the succession of supreme pontiffs and in the dignified and sensitive person of Benedict XVI. It is to him, who is worthy of deep appreciation for his simple yet strong courage in his service, that I declare my respectful communion and express my deep love.

Giuseppe Agostino
Metropolitan Archbishop Emeritus
Cosenza–Bisignano, Italy

the WORD among us®

The *Spirit* of Catholic Living

This book was published by The Word Among Us. Since 1981, The Word Among Us has been answering the call of the Second Vatican Council to help Catholic laypeople encounter Christ in the Scriptures.

The name of our company comes from the prologue to the Gospel of John and reflects the vision and purpose of all of our publications: to be an instrument of the Spirit, whose desire is to manifest Jesus' presence in and to the children of God. In this way, we hope to contribute to the Church's ongoing mission of proclaiming the gospel to the world so that all people would know the love and mercy of our Lord and grow ever more deeply in love with him.

Our monthly devotional magazine, *The Word Among Us*, features meditations on the daily and Sunday Mass readings, and currently reaches more than one million Catholics in North America and another half million Catholics in one hundred countries around the world. Our book division, The Word Among Us Press, publishes numerous books, Bible studies, and pamphlets that help Catholics grow in their faith.

To learn more about who we are and what we publish, log on to our website at www.wau.org. There you will find a variety of Catholic resources that will help you grow in your faith.

Embrace His Word, Listen to God . . .

www.wau.org